MW00414080

How to Evangelize

Bringing Back the Gospel

Thomas W. Bear

Acknowledgments

I wish to thank my wife Linda and my friend, David McMillin for their strong encouragement to write this book and help with its improvement. I thank Elaine Burke and Natalie Hays for their extensive help in the editing process. I also thank my brother Michael Bear, Sarah Jakubiec, Kendall Scott, Bernie Wright, Eric Moore, Patrick McMahon and Scott Cherry for all of their contributions.

How to Evangelize: Bringing Back the Gospel

Copyright 2017 by Thomas W. Bear
22433 Oxford St.
Dearborn, MI 48124

All rights reserved. No part of this publication may be reproduced, or transmitted in any form by any means, electronic, mechanical, photocopy, recording or otherwise, without the prior permission of the publisher, except as provided by USA copyright law.

Printed in the United States of America

Unless otherwise noted, all Bible quotations are taken from the HOLY BIBLE, NEW INTERNATIONAL VERSION® . Copyright© 1973, 1978, 1984, by International Bible Society. Used by permission of Zondervan Publishing House. All rights reserved.

The "NIV" and "New International Version" trademarks are registered in the United States Patent and Trademark Office by International Bible Society. Use of either trademark requires the permission of the International Bible Society.

Any Scripture taken from the New American Standard Bible®, Copyright © 1960, 1962, 1963, 1968, 1972, 1973, 1975, 1977, 1995 by the Lockman Foundation. Used by permission and noted by the abbreviation "NASB."

Contents

Introduction

For almost twenty years, I have been engaged in purposeful evangelism outings on a weekly basis. I have had gospel conversations with thousands of people from every continent except Antarctica. I have also conducted many evangelism seminars aimed at equipping Christians to evangelize. During this period, I have continually examined my understanding of evangelism against the biblical record. I wanted my understanding and practices to be patterned after that of Jesus and His Apostles.

My understanding of evangelism has undergone much refinement during the past twenty years. Though some may disagree, I believe that all of my study and experience during these years has produced expertise that can benefit others who want to learn how to evangelize according to the pattern observed in the Bible. I have written this book hoping to help Christians who sincerely want to learn how to evangelize like Jesus and His Apostles.

Let me tell you up front that some of the information in this book will likely go against the grain of your current understanding of evangelism. When you come across a statement that does not fit your understanding of evangelism, do not assume that it is false just because you have not heard it before. I am not a lone voice. Many men have written similar things in centuries past. I believe that if men like Charles Spurgeon and Jonathan Edwards were alive today and read this book, they would be in full agreement with it. If you consider yourself a serious student of the Bible and you read this book prayerfully, I believe you will be challenged, encouraged and better equipped to do the work of evangelism.

To prepare you for the work of evangelism, **Section 1** surveys the New Testament to establish the message and methods that the apostles and Jesus used to make disciples. **Section 2** presents principles gleaned from this survey to help you go and do the work of evangelism. These principles cover the various phases of making disciples from the initial proclamation of the gospel, to discerning when a disciple is made and concluding with what must take place once disciples are made. The more you attempt to put these principles into practice, the more resistance you should expect from forces opposed to Jesus. **Section 3** examines the type of opposition you should expect. **Section 4** analyzes the importance of prayer for all who engage in this work. Lastly, a variety of supporting instruction is provided in the **Appendixes**, including some examples of actual documented gospel conversations.

Note: This book involves mainly instruction about evangelism. My book, *Evangelism Fuel, Motivation to Evangelize* was written to provide reasons why we should evangelize and encouragement to do it.

Section 1: Preparing for the Work of Evangelism

- Develop an increasingly purposeful evangelistic mindset.

- Refine your understanding of evangelism.

- Prepare your heart.

"If a man could see himself as the Holy God sees him, he would gladly believe the gospel and bow his knee to Jesus."

"Until a man gets a glimpse of himself as the Holy God sees him, he simply will not come to Christ."

Tom Bear

Develop an increasingly purposeful evangelistic mindset.

Jesus told us to go and make disciples from people of all nations and to teach them to observe all the things He commanded (Matthew 28:18-20). Before He ascended to heaven, Jesus also said that we would be witnesses of Him to the uttermost parts of the world (Acts 1:8). It is possible to be a witness without being purposeful about it. For example, we could be walking down the street singing a song of praise to God while unaware that an unbeliever is watching and listening. Or, we could be praying softly with a heart of thankfulness affirming God's goodness in the face of great adversity unaware that an unbeliever is observing us. In these examples, we could have been witnessing unto Christ even though we were not aware that we were doing so. Therefore, it is possible at any given moment to be witnesses unto Jesus without necessarily being purposely engaged in the work of "making disciples."

To follow Jesus' command **to go** and "make disciples",[1] we must do so purposefully. The Bible teaches that the intentional work of presenting the gospel is the primary means for making disciples. Paul stated, *"The gospel is THE power of God unto salvation to everyone who believes"* *(Romans 1:16)*. To fulfill Jesus' command to go and make disciples, we must be about the purposeful proclamation of the Gospel. If we do not do this, disciples will not be made.

Let me ask you an important question. **Is it your goal to purposefully, and regularly communicate the gospel so that disciples are made?** Stop and think about this question. Take an honest look inward and evaluate if this is an active, ongoing goal of yours. You may not have much knowledge or experience in evangelism. But if you never come to the place in your life where you make it your lifelong goal to make disciples, you should not expect God to use you in this way. You will not be inclined to learn how to evangelize. You will not be inclined to purposely engage in gospel conversations. As a result, you will not make many disciples.

Let me challenge you to begin aggressively asking God to develop in you the mindset that He wants you to possess about making disciples. This is not something I can teach you. God must form it in you and He is pleased to do so for all who desperately ask Him.

[1] When I use the term "make disciples," I am not suggesting that we have the power to actually make them. We sow the gospel seed and water the gospel seed. Ultimately, God is the one who causes the gospel seed to spring to life.

If you seriously follow my challenge and continue to do so throughout your life, the scope of evangelism will broaden in your mind and heart. If you are like most evangelically ambitious Christians that I have known, you possess some excitement for spreading the gospel. But God wants to broaden the scope in you to include the actual making of disciples, not merely the proclamation of the gospel itself. I have noticed that most ambitious evangelistic Christians are content to simply proclaim the gospel audibly or through gospel literature. They think that their job is complete once the gospel has been communicated to an unbeliever. Let me stress that this is merely the beginning of the work. It is highly unusual for people to truly embrace Jesus after hearing the gospel for the first time.[2]

You must consider the unbelievers you meet as future potential followers of Jesus who will need ongoing care. We must be willing to continue visiting and teaching them. We must be willing to intercede for them, pleading with God to cause the gospel seed to spring to life. We must also never conclude that the person is a follower of Jesus if there is no fruit of repentance. The goal is not to get people to pray sinner's prayers. The goal is changed lives, followers of Jesus who regularly gather with other followers of Jesus.

---

[2] Unfortunately, some Christians wrongly conclude a person becomes a follower of Jesus as a result of praying a sinner's prayer. They conclude that their work of evangelizing was successful and complete because they constructed dialog that resulted in the unbeliever praying a sinner's prayer. Virtually none of the people who pray a sinner's prayer then begin to follow Jesus Christ. Not only is the job of evangelizing incomplete, it is often harmed. The person goes away thinking he is a Christian with nothing to worry about at the judgment. When they do not observe any difference in their life afterward, they conclude that the gospel claim is not real. Or, worse, they assume that they are "saved" and heaven bound. I call this evangelism malpractice and very dangerous. It certainly is not a practice taught in the New Testament! For more on this, refer to Appendix B.

If these truths are not already firmly engrafted into your very soul, please begin asking God to help you see these things as He sees them. Once you do, you will recognize more than ever that the work of evangelism is impossible, humanly speaking. As you meet people and proclaim the gospel to them, you will begin praying diligently for their souls. And you will learn all the more that you cannot make them alive. God has to do this. They only thing you can do is pray. And when some of these people suddenly lose interest causing you to become discouraged, you will learn all the more that without Jesus, you can do nothing. This work requires large faith.

If all you do right now is proclaim the gospel and walk away, your faith is not being stretched. But if you see the job as incomplete until the unbeliever is raised to new life and walking in fellowship with God's people, you will be forced to get on your knees and keep asking God to do the impossible. This is like asking God to move a literal mountain into the sea. But it is something He calls us to do.

May God expand your current understanding of evangelism until you embrace the fact that you are called to do work that is humanly impossible. The more God causes this mindset to develop within you, the more useful you will be in His Kingdom.

Refine your understanding of evangelism.

A faithful steward not only carries out his responsibilities, he strives to do it in a way that most honors his master. To please his master, he carefully does his job as instructed by his master. God has entrusted the work of advancing His Kingdom to all believers. This makes us stewards. It is only fitting, therefore, that we learn how to evangelize as instructed by our Master. We should naturally desire to become most useful and effective. This does not mean that brand new believers should wait to evangelize. On the contrary, all Christians are called to be witnesses no matter how long they have known the Lord. Yet, in our desire to honor the Lord, we should make up our minds to become increasingly proficient at proclaiming the gospel, for HIS NAME'S SAKE. We must study and learn our Master's instructions. To honor our Master, we must be willing to conform the way we evangelize to His instructions rather than what seems best to us.

If you desire to evangelize like Jesus and the apostles, you will most likely have to refine your understanding of evangelism to some degree. Since the Bible is our most important resource, this book carefully examines how Jesus and His apostles evangelized. This examination is provided to help the sincere Bible student begin the process of abandoning unbiblical views about evangelism.

Know the major barrier to the gospel.

Immediately after my conversion, I could not wait to tell all my friends the gospel. I was sure they would all want to be saved. I was shocked when they rejected it. Why did they reject it? I know now that it was because their hearts were darkened. *"For although they knew God, they neither glorified him as God nor gave thanks to him, but their thinking became futile and their foolish **hearts were darkened**" (Romans 1:21).* Because God enlightened my heart, the gospel was suddenly glorious to me. But my friends were still unable to see the glory of the gospel because their hearts remained darkened. I also know now that the real problem was their hearts, not their intellect. *"For it is with your **heart** that you believe and are justified" (Romans 10:10).*

If you speak with enough unbelievers, you will see that the most blatant symptom of a darkened heart is an inability to see oneself rightly and to see God rightly. People believe they are not that bad and that God's standard of righteousness is less than absolute. They are good in their own eyes, at least better than many "wicked" people who have committed crimes such as murder. They think, "Surely, I am not bad enough to warrant everlasting punishment in hell." They turn a blind eye toward their own sin and take refuge in the false notion that God will accept them on the basis of their own goodness. The New Testament demonstrates that Jesus and His apostles understood that due to their darkened hearts, unbelievers cannot see themselves or God rightly. This understanding affected the way Jesus and His apostles evangelized.

It has been about two thousand years since Jesus issued the great commission to go and make disciples of all nations. These days, Christians generally believe that the good news of Jesus Christ should be presented in a manner that is not offensive to the hearer. Most think it is inappropriate to use gospel presentation methods that mention much about sin and hell. Evangelists that use them are often thought of as "hellfire and brimstone" preachers. What image comes to your mind when you hear the phrase "hellfire and brimstone preacher?" For many Christians, such a description likely produces an image of a scowling, judgmental man that yells at people and does all that he can to "scare them into the Kingdom." I think most of us would agree that Christians should be joyful, compassionate people that reflect the beauty of Christ. Surely we are supposed to be lights that shine in the darkness, not people who appear filled with hate and rage. But some have wrongly concluded that to be consistent with our desire to win people to Christ through a loving, positive influence, we should avoid words and methods that tend to put people in a negative mindset toward us. They think, "How will people ever be won to Christ if we turn them off even before they have a chance to hear the good news?"

Several years ago, a Christian brother told me that unless the hearer is troubled or bothered by what he is hearing in my gospel presentation, then I am failing to proclaim the entire gospel to him. I remember reacting negatively toward what my Christian friend had to say. Like most Christians, I believed it was my primary duty to talk about the "good news" of forgiveness through Christ and not focus so much on things like sin and judgment. Subsequently, I began noticing how people were responding to what I was telling them and began to realize that the "good news" was coming across as irrelevant. The hearers seemed apathetic toward it.

I began to realize that while I had good intentions to lovingly proclaim the good news of Jesus Christ to those around me, I was failing to fulfill my responsibility to really love them. If I behold a blind man walking on a bridge that has been washed out ahead of him and it is apparent that he is unaware of the pending danger, it is my responsibility to warn him. Failing to do so would be hateful and tantamount to murder or at least manslaughter.

I resolved that I must learn how to present the full gospel of Jesus with a heart of sincere love for the hearers but to do it in such a way that they might better understand their actual predicament. Now when I evangelize, I do so with a strong determination to help the hearer perceive his actual condition before I tell him about the remedy. I continue talking about sin and judgment until I perceive that the person gains a mental comprehension of his predicament. I want him to understand that the wrath of God is resting on him (John 3:36) so that when I explain God's plan of salvation through Christ, he sees the reason for Jesus' death in his behalf. As you will discover in this section of the book, this is precisely what Jesus and His apostles did in order to prepare the hearers for the good news. Following their example has been eye opening for me because I have seen with my own eyes how these principles really work.

They reasoned about sin, righteousness and judgment

A brief survey of the New Testament will show **that in order to properly convey the gospel, Jesus and the apostles always spoke about sin, righteousness and judgment as THE means to prepare hearts to receive the gospel seed.** Until you embrace this principle, your understanding of evangelism will not be formed in accordance with the biblical pattern. I am fully convinced that anyone who does not purposely reason with people about sin, righteousness and judgment, or merely skims over these issues, WILL FAIL to present the gospel the way Jesus and the apostles presented it.

Before beginning this discussion, let me address a common misconception that seems to keep many people from taking an honest look at these matters. Some would suggest that if a person insists on discussing issues like sin, righteousness and judgment, he is an unloving person who knows nothing about the love of God. Jonathan Edwards lived about two hundred years ago and taught many of the things you will read in this book. His most famous sermon was titled, *"Sinners in the Hands of an Angry God."* It was perhaps the most famous sermon ever delivered in the U.S. In it he spoke much of sin, righteousness and judgment. Many people took offense at some of the things he said and to this day some ridicule him and think he was just an angry man whose God was an angry God. This same man said, *"The work of redemption which the gospel makes known, above all things affords motives to love; for that work was the most glorious and wonderful exhibition of love that ever was seen or heard of.* **Love is the principle thing that the gospel dwells on when speaking of God, and of Christ."** [3] Do these sound like words of an angry, scowling man? I agree with Edwards that the gospel can be summed up in the word LOVE. Yet, I maintain that it is impossible to properly convey the wonders of Christ's love without first discussing the realities of sin, righteousness and judgment.

I don't want to give the impression that I intentionally offend people with Bible truth only to make them miserable. I can assure you from much experience that it is possible to talk with people about such subjects with a heart full of compassion.

---

[3] Edwards, Jonathan, Charity and its Fruits, The Banner of Truth Trust, Carlisle, PA, 2000. p. 19

Paul reasoned about sin, righteousness and judgment.

The Apostle Paul is considered by most Bible believers to be the greatest evangelist and missionary that ever lived. God used Paul to spread the gospel and plant churches throughout the civilized world of his day. Paul often urged his readers to imitate his ways. He claimed that the message he preached was the word of God and commended the Thessalonians for receiving it as such and spreading it throughout the region of Macedonia and Achaia (I Thessalonians 2:13 & 1:8). It logically follows that if we preach the same message and do it after the manner of Paul, we will be doing it in the way that God desires.

In the book of Acts, Luke noted that Paul was in the habit of "reasoning" with both Jews and Gentiles, trying to persuade them. Often, he did this in synagogues. In Athens, he did it in the market place "day by day," and in Ephesus he did it publicly from "house to house." (See Acts 17:2-4, 17:17, 18:1-4, 18:19, 20:20-21.) How did Paul reason with his hearers? According to I Corinthians 2:1, Paul's message and his preaching was, *"Not with wise and persuasive words, but with a demonstration of the Spirit's power, so that the faith of the hearer's might not rest on men's wisdom, but on God's power."* What did Paul reason with his hearers about? The content of Paul's message is summarized in his statement, ***"We preach Christ crucified**: a stumbling block to Jews and foolishness to Gentiles"* (I Corinthians 1:23). Let us now consider the biblical record in order to gain a fuller comprehension of what Paul preached in order to make disciples. In the book of Acts, Luke said that Paul's message included the following:

- <u>A call to repent</u>: *I have declared to both Jews and Greeks that they must **turn to God in repentance** and have faith in our Lord Jesus (Acts 20:21). "first to those in Damascus, then to those in Jerusalem and in all Judea, and to the Gentiles also, I preached **that <u>they should repent</u> and turn to God** and **prove their repentance by their deeds"** (Acts 26:20).*

- <u>Teaching about why the Christ had to suffer</u>: *"I am saying nothing beyond what the prophets and Moses said would happen-- **that the Christ would suffer** and, as the first to rise from the dead, would proclaim light to his own people and to the Gentiles"* (Acts 26:22-23).

- <u>Discourse about righteousness, self-control and judgment</u>: ***"Paul discoursed about righteousness, self-control and judgment to come"*** *(Acts 24:25).*

- Teaching about the Kingdom of God: *"From morning till evening Paul explained and **declared to them the Kingdom of God** and tried to convince them about Jesus from the Law of Moses and from the Prophets"* (Acts 28:23).

As we will see later, Luke's record of Paul's message is consistent with the letters Paul wrote and also with the message that Jesus preached. But before moving on, let us consider some of the phrases Luke recorded to glean further understanding of Paul's message.

Turn to God in repentance- Consider the word "repentance." This word is used throughout the New Testament. John the Baptist, Jesus and the apostles used it. It means essentially to stop going one way and go the opposite way. It implies that the hearer is going the wrong way and needs to turn and go the opposite direction. Those who used the word repent or repentance were calling attention to something negative about the hearer. The hearer was living a life that was wrong in God's sight and must turn completely around to avoid judgment. From this phrase we know that the message of Jesus and His apostles pointed out that something was wrong about the lives of their hearers.

That the Christ would suffer- Admittedly, Paul had to spend much time proving to the Jews that the Christ would suffer. They were expecting that when the Christ arrived, He would usher in a new kingdom on earth that would crush the Roman Empire. So, Paul simply quoted Old Testament scriptures to prove that the Christ would suffer. But eventually, Paul would have to reason with the hearers as to **why** the Christ had to suffer. In his epistles, Paul does this very thing by pointing to the depravity of all mankind and their just condemnation (See Romans 1:18-2:2, 3:10-21; Galatians 3:19-22; Ephesians 2:1-3; Colossians 1:13-14, 21-22; II Thessalonians 1:7-9). According to these verses, Paul preached the following things:

- All people are born into the kingdom of darkness that is ruled by Satan. Being aligned with Satan under his rule, all people are born into the world alienated from God and are His enemies.

- In order for His enemies to have peace declared between themselves and God, they have to be reconciled on His terms.

- These terms require full punishment for all crimes that God's enemies commit against Him.

- Since the enemies of God can never make up for their crimes, they will have to either suffer eternally away from the holy God or receive a perfect right standing through a qualified, sinless substitute who suffered in their place for all the crimes they committed. God Himself became that sacrifice and this is the only sacrifice that satisfies His righteous demands.

In order to reason with his hearers as to why the Christ had to suffer, Paul taught them these things. His teaching did not shy away from identifying the absolute wretchedness found in every man. He did not make God out to be an unrighteous Judge that can simply sweep the sins of His enemies under the carpet. Rather, Paul taught that God has appointed a day that He will judge the world through Jesus Christ and cast all the unbelievers into everlasting torment.

Righteousness, self-control and judgment to come- We can glean more about Paul's methods and message from Luke's record of Paul's hearing with Felix.

> *"Several days later Felix came with his wife Drusilla, who was a Jewess. He sent for Paul and listened to him as he spoke about faith in Christ Jesus. As Paul discoursed on righteousness, self-control and the judgment to come, Felix was afraid and said, "That's enough for now! You may leave. When I find it convenient, I will send for you." (Acts 24:24-25).*

According to Luke's record in Acts, part of Paul's dialog about faith in Christ Jesus included subjects like "righteousness, self-control and judgment to come." From the testimony in Acts, we get the impression that Paul's captors had a high respect for him. This suggests that he must not have acted like a scowling "fire and brimstone preacher" pictured in so many Hollywood movies. We get the impression that it is possible to discuss subjects like hell, sin, and righteousness in an intelligent, sincere and loving manner. Paul did not "look down" in judgment on his hearers or "rant and rave" at them. Nevertheless, it is easy to prove that he spoke about things that were undoubtedly offensive to them.

Declared to them the Kingdom of God- Implied in the phrase, "Kingdom of God," is the concept of authority. In a kingdom, the king has absolute authority over his subjects. Those living in democratic countries have difficulty feeling the weight of this. We have no concept of what it is like to live under the absolute rule of a sovereign king. If we did, we might have a greater sense of fear toward God as the One who has absolute authority over His subjects. We might understand better just how dangerous it is to offend such a King. When Paul and Jesus preached the Kingdom of God, the hearers understood these things because such rule existed in most human governments of the day.

Paul's writings reveal his "message."- To learn more about the message Paul preached, we can simply read his letter to the Romans. Paul wrote this letter to people that he had not previously met in order to convey the gospel in great detail to them. In this epistle, Paul "reasons" with the reader using various biblical texts to establish his case. To imitate Paul, we should strive to convey the same message in a manner that impacts those who listen as Paul's letter impacted those who received it. Does Paul's letter to the Romans contain arguments designed to prove the existence of God and authority of His word? No! On the contrary, he merely states as fact that God has already declared everything people need to know through the creation so that any who deny His existence are without excuse. Also, rather than debate the authority of the Bible, he attributes complete authority to it by the way he quotes from it as The Word of God.

Let us now consider how his message, as laid out for us in his letter to the Romans, would impact the hearer or reader. In the first section (1:1 through 3:20), Paul argues from Old Testament scripture that all people are natural born enemies of God, wicked in His sight and justly condemned and fully deserving of His wrath. Paul does not beat around the bush or sugar coat this message. He quotes from various Old Testament scriptures to establish truths such as those that follow:

- Absolutely no one "seeks God" (3:11).
- There is absolutely no one that qualifies as "good" in God's sight (3:10 & 12).
- In themselves, everyone is useless for God's purposes (3:12).
- All people are liars by nature (3:13).
- It is the nature of people to murder (3:15).

- All people of the world are justly condemned and accountable to God for their actions (3:9 & 19).

All of the gospel themes that Paul discusses from 3:21 to the end of the book are based upon the foundation first laid in 1:1 – 3:20. In other words, when Paul reasoned with people about Jesus, he obviously considered it essential to first get personal with them about their sin and prove that they deserved condemnation before discussing God's chosen remedy as seen in the substitutionary death of Jesus. Paul was guided by the truth that Jesus came to save sinners, not those who think they can come before God based upon their own righteousness. (See Luke 5:31-32.)

Jesus reasoned about sin, righteousness and judgment.

Our consideration of Jesus' teachings will serve to underscore why Paul and the other apostles spent so much time discussing sin, righteousness and judgment to come.

The world has always had its philosophers who, like the Athenians, spent *"their time doing nothing but talking about and listening to the latest ideas" (Acts 17:21).* They pride themselves in their ability to reason with their minds supposing to understand the meaning of life. But Jesus, the Creator of life, is the meaning of life. Jesus' teachings were unlike those of any man that had lived before Him. In contrast to a mere man, *"He taught as one who had authority" (Matthew 7:29).* As the Great Physician, He understood the sickness of the human heart. He said, *"Out of the heart come evil thoughts, murder, adultery, sexual immorality, theft, false testimony, slander" (Matthew 15:19).* When He made statements like this, He spoke them as if He was the Physician that has the knowledge and ability to heal, not as one who also was in need of healing. You and I can quote Matthew 15:19 to others to help them better understand the condition of the hearts of all people, including our own. But Jesus spoke these words as if they were coming directly from the mouth of God. He spoke as One having authority and as the One who "looks at the heart." (See I Samuel 16:7 and John 2:25.)

As we consider how Jesus made disciples, keep in mind that, being the Great Physician, He always sought to cut into the hearts of His listeners. If you read the gospels with this in mind, you will note that much of His teachings dealt with the sinfulness of man and the righteousness of God in order to sweep away the lie that each man loves to believe- the lie that he is righteous enough to stand before God. Jesus said, *"It is not the healthy who need a doctor, but the sick. I have not come to call the righteous, but sinners to repentance" (Luke 5:31-32).*

For a man to become a disciple of Jesus, he must first be stripped of the lie that he has been clinging to and see himself as one who has greatly offended God as a wicked criminal headed for punishment. When Jesus talked with them, He spoke about things that would help people gain this type of understanding and eventually embrace it in their hearts. In order to become more effective evangelists, we must follow the pattern of Jesus and His disciples. Consider some examples of how Jesus spoke words that would help people better understand their sinful condition before the righteous God.

One of my favorite examples is Jesus' conversation with the Samaritan woman in the fourth chapter of John's gospel. First, we notice that Jesus loved this sinner. It made no difference to Him that she was a woman or that she was a Samaritan. The Jews considered Samaritans inferior. Jewish men generally did not speak with Samaritans. To top it off, this one was a woman.

Jesus saw her as one who was alienated from God and in need of reconciliation. His love drove Him to speak words to her that would result in her salvation. He does not quickly hit her with the fact that she is a rebel against God. First, He speaks of something for which her soul longs-living water that springs up to eternal life. For the first part of the conversation, she remains fixed in her self-righteousness without facing her need of salvation. It was in a state of unbelief that she said, *"Sir, give me this water so that I won't get thirsty and have to keep coming here to draw water."* Her statement seems to have a sarcastic tone. She really didn't believe what Jesus had said to her.

Knowing that the woman was refusing to see herself rightly, Jesus then confronted her with her own sinful life. She had been married several times and was currently living with a man out of wedlock. This pricked her heart and made her feel uncomfortable. So, she began to squirm and tried to get the focus off her sinfulness. But Jesus continued the dialog with more foundational truth. From this narrative, we observe that once He got her attention by talking about the living water, Jesus began working the soil of her heart by tilling it with truth about her sinfulness.

After His words reminded her of her sinfulness, He introduced Himself as the Messiah. Then, faith sprang to life in the Samaritan woman and she immediately began testifying to her neighbors with spontaneous excitement that she had found the Messiah. (See John 4:7-30.) It is in this immediate context that Jesus instructs His disciples to go into the harvest and reap as He was reaping.

To prepare the soil of the human heart so that people would understand their sinful condition, Jesus often spoke in parables knowing that those parables would benefit some people and not others. For example, He used the parable of the Pharisee and the tax collector to teach that only those who see themselves as the wretched tax collector in need of God's mercy can be justified. (See Luke 18:9-14.) By identifying the repentant tax collector as the one who was justified before God, He disturbed those who were trusting in their own righteousness.

Jesus often used the law to confront people with God's righteousness so that they might begin to see themselves rightly. For example, a lawyer once asked him what he must do to inherit eternal life. Rather than answering the way we would answer, Jesus said, *"What is written in the Law? How do you read it?"* The lawyer answered, *"Love the Lord your God with all your heart and with all your soul and with all your strength and with all your mind"*; and, *"Love your neighbor as yourself."* Then Jesus said, *"You have answered correctly, do this and you will live"* (Luke 10:25-28). Rather than tell the lawyer that all his righteous deeds were as filthy rags, He simply applied the law to the man's heart.

Jesus knew that this man (like all unbelievers) was seeing himself as righteous enough. Perhaps the man was bothered and wanted some reassurance that he was acceptable to God, so he asked, *"And who is my neighbor?"* (The Bible says that he wanted to justify himself.) Then Jesus proceeded to tell him a parable about a Samaritan who acted in a loving manner toward a man who was left injured and dying. In this discourse, Jesus still did not present the lawyer with the "good news." He confronted him with the very law that the man was counting on to make himself right with God. Jesus merely said, *"Go and do likewise."* Jesus was using the law to show to this man that he was failing to measure up to God's righteousness.

From Jesus' command to go and do likewise we can deduce that the man had been failing to act in the way that the Samaritan treated the injured man. Not only this, the lawyer was probably thinking of himself as far superior to all Samaritans. While we would want to take this opportunity to proclaim the good news of the forgiveness of sins through Jesus' sacrificial death, Jesus was content to leave this man without explaining it to him. It appears that Jesus did not think that this ground was quite ready for the gospel seed to be planted.

Jesus used the law in a similar way when confronting the rich young ruler who also saw himself as righteous. (See Luke 18:18-23.) Jesus confronted him with the law and the young man said that he had kept it all his life. Rather than tell him he was self-deceived, Jesus merely said, *"Go and sell all your possessions and give them to the poor and then come and follow me."* By saying this, Jesus revealed to this man that he was failing to keep the law. He was covetous. To fulfill the law, we must love others as ourselves. This man loved himself more than others because he would not share his wealth with anyone. The man went away miserable because he recognized that he loved his riches too much to let go of them.

This exchange showed that he really did not believe in his heart that he needed salvation. Otherwise, he would have followed Jesus' advice. He got a glimpse of his wretchedness. The rich young ruler was not willing to let go of the life he loved so much. And according to Jesus, a man must "lose his own life" in order to inherit eternal life. (See Matthew 10:39, 16:25, Mark 8:35, Luke 9:24, 17:33.)

Besides these things, Jesus taught the following:

- All people are born wretched sinners with hearts full of murder and adultery (Matthew 15:10-20, John 8:44).
- People need to repent. *"**From that time on** Jesus began to preach, "Repent, for the Kingdom of heaven is near" (Matthew 4:17).*
- Judgment is coming and all deserve to be cast into hell (Matthew 5:22, 29-30; 7:21-23; 8:12; 10:28; 13:37-50; 22:13; 25:30; Luke13:24-30; 14:16;16:19-31).
- Unless a person lets go of the life he loves so much, he will not inherit eternal life (Matthew 10:39).
- A person must be willing to die for Jesus (Matt.16:24-28).
- All true believers will be hated by the world (Matthew 10:22-23; John 15:20-25).

Jesus and His apostles taught and preached about the Kingdom of God. This kingdom is the opposite of the kingdom of darkness. All things pertaining to the Kingdom of light are offensive to the subjects in the kingdom of darkness. Being in darkness, the people are blinded by their king Satan (II Corinthians 4:4). In order to help people begin to see, we must follow the pattern of Jesus and His apostles. People need to be lovingly confronted with their true condition before God and warned that all His enemies will rightly be thrown into eternal hell at the coming judgment. Just as Jesus did not skip over these matters, we too must be willing to discuss them. One of our goals must be to help the hearer understand his condition before God and we should be willing to take as much time and be as direct as necessary in order to accomplish it. He must begin to see the vileness of his sin in God's sight.

Suggestion: Try reading the book of Matthew again taking special notice of how Jesus interacted with people. This reading will underscore what I have written here.

How did Jesus and the apostles proclaim the "good news?"

If you have read up to this point, you probably know by now that, from my perspective, proclaiming the good news of Jesus Christ is something far different than saying, "Smile. God loves you." We must talk about things that may seem negative. Yet, for every negative point we make about sin, righteousness and judgment, there is a positive counter point in the good news of Jesus Christ.

Examples:

- We must tell them that no one is righteous. But we can also tell them that whoever believes from the heart receive a righteousness from God that is not their own.

- We must tell them that because God is absolutely righteous, He must punish each and every sin. But we can also tell them that Jesus took all of the punishment we deserve for each and every sin.

- We must tell them that all people are rebels against the rule of God. But we can also tell them that when God raises a person to new life and reconciles him to Himself, He causes him to gladly discard his own ambitions and self-rule to take upon himself the yoke of our new, loving and wise Master who can be fully trusted to rule over his life. The salvation Jesus offers includes not only the deliverance from the penalty of sin which is hell, it also brings about deliverance from slavery to sin because He causes His life to be inside of us.

- We must tell them that people live selfish lives and tend to hurt each other. But we can also tell them that when God delivers a man out of darkness, He gives him a new heart that seeks the welfare of others above his own. He makes us to become more and more like Jesus.

Only when a man comprehends the vastness of his sin and God's perfect righteousness will he begin to fathom the fullness of the good news of Jesus Christ. To proclaim the gospel properly, we should make much of both the bad news and the good news so that the hearer perceives the connection between the elements of each. The more the hearer understands the various facets of the bad news, the more he will comprehend the love of God as seen in the sacrifice of His Son in his behalf. If you have explained the bad news in great detail, then you will be able to proclaim the good news in great detail. It is with great joy that we can exclaim glorious truths like those below:

- Though we were enemies of God deserving nothing but His wrath, God sent His Son into the world to take our punishment for us! (Isaiah 53:6).

- Two thousand years ago, Jesus was whipped, beaten and hung on a cross to die even though He had never sinned. He took our sins upon Himself and bore the wrath of God as our substitute (I Peter 3:18).

- This voluntary, obedient sacrifice satisfied the righteous demands of God. Justice was served (Romans 3:21-26).

- Whoever places their trust in Jesus as the only way to be reconciled to God and believes that Jesus' sacrifice satisfied God's righteous demands, receives remission[4] of sins, once and for all (Acts 10:43).

- Jesus was not defeated. Through His death, He gained victory for God! (Colossians 2:15). On the third day after His death, Jesus rose from the dead and was seen by many witnesses. Then God raised Him up to sit at His right hand as Lord and Judge over all (Acts 17:31).

- Jesus will re-create the heavens and the earth where His people will enjoy Him forever, and all who do not know Him will be cast into hell forever (Revelation 21:1-8).

- God has made the way open for all who believe to be reconciled to Him and to begin following Jesus as the new loving Master over their lives (John 3:16).

- In addition to deliverance from the penalty of sin, we are delivered from slavery to sin. We become more and more like Jesus Himself. (Romans 6:18, Romans 8:29)

---

[4] In this book, I purposely use the phrase "remission of sins" rather than "forgiveness of sins." See Appendix H for a full explanation of my reason.

Their conversations usually involved two-way dialog.

In the gospels, we often see Jesus speaking with a single person. In many of these instances, there were others standing around observing but most of his recorded dialog was one-on-one. Jesus, the Lord of heaven and earth, evidently saw value in purposely speaking with people one-on-one. He whose time was worth more than the universe itself, thought it was important to spend time speaking with people one-on-one. This should be our attitude also. If Jesus took the time to do it, then so should we. Beyond the example Jesus set for us, we should do so because these conversations afford opportunities to discuss the gospel using two-way dialog, which is the most efficient means for presenting the gospel.

When the gospel is proclaimed to larger groups without two-way dialog, the people listen, but only with varying degrees of attentiveness. In this type of setting, the unbeliever can more easily be distracted and thus miss much of what is being said. He is also prone to think that he is not the sinner being addressed by the preacher. When we talk face-to-face with an unbeliever, he is a captive audience. In one-on-one conversations, both parties involved must listen and comprehend what each other is saying or the conversation essentially comes to a halt. Each person must concentrate on what the other person is saying so that he will be able to answer or ask a question or share something relevant to the next statement he hears.

During a mission exposure trip to Minneapolis in the summer of 2008, our team visited a soup kitchen that ministers to the downcast. During this meeting, the gospel was accurately and faithfully presented and then a meal was served. During the meal time, I met Lester, a Native American homeless man in his late twenties. Lester seemed bright and was quite articulate as we discussed the gospel.

During this conversation, I learned that Lester had attended many of these meetings in the past and had heard the gospel proclaimed on numerous occasions. He said he had accepted Jesus a few years earlier, but most of the words he spoke to me suggested otherwise. I asked him if he thought he was a good person. He said "Yes." I asked him if he had heard the Ten Commandments. He said, "Yes." I asked him if he had kept them. He said, "Pretty much... perhaps seven or eight of them." In his mind, keeping most of them meant he was good. He was relying on his relative goodness for hope of heaven.

For several minutes, I began teaching him more about God's standard of righteousness. He was surprised to learn that hating someone was the same as murdering them in our heart. He said he had often hated people including even his own mother and father. Then I taught him that each time a man sins, he commits idolatry because he puts himself in God's place as ruler and thus makes himself out to be god over his life. He understood this. I also taught him that God's absolute righteousness demands that all sin be punished. I showed him that all people fully deserve hell and that if a person dies with their sin, they will go there forever.

As a result of our two-way discussion, Lester seemed to be awakened to the seriousness of his condition for the first time. Lester had attended many meetings prior to our discussion during which the gospel was preached to larger groups of people. Our one-on-one discussion proved more effective in Lester's case.

I have had many other conversations with people like Lester. They all had heard the gospel before but until they were involved in a one-on-one conversation that forced them to personally interact about the gospel, they never really understood its ramifications for their lives.

Besides all this, face-to-face conversations enable us to observe the body language and facial expressions of the person with whom we are talking. We can judge better if the gospel message is getting through because it produces reaction in the hearer.

We conclude that the gospel is most effectively conveyed using two-way dialog and preferably one-on-one. Is it any wonder why this seems to be the most common method that was employed by Jesus and the apostles?

Methods <u>not</u> used by Jesus and the apostles

They did not gather people together to hear them preach.

What picture comes to your mind when you envision an evangelist? Do you see a man on television? Do you see a man standing at a podium in front of a large crowd? I suspect that many Christians consider Billy Graham the world's greatest evangelist. He spoke to very large gatherings of people. Prior to him, evangelists held similar crusades using tent meetings. This practice has been continued to this day. Many churches hold periodic "revivals" in their church building. Evangelists are invited to speak at these meetings that often extend over several days. Let's face it, most evangelism approaches attempt to gather as many people as possible together where the gospel message can be delivered. While this may be a valid way to reach people with the gospel, it does not seem to be something practiced by Jesus or His Apostles.

Jesus never made efforts to gather crowds together in order to speak to them. When crowds of people did hear the word preached, it was God who gathered them together, not the apostles. The evangelists in the New Testament did not utilize a strategy of gathering people together to hear a "professional" preach the gospel. Sometimes, Paul purposefully went to places where there would be people already gathered together. Since it was his commission to preach to the Jews first, then to the Gentiles, he often went to synagogues. But his strategy never included efforts on his part to gather people together beforehand.

Most Christians relegate evangelism to the professionals. They are content to be spectators rather than participants. Instead of recognizing God's call for them to evangelize, they might occasionally invite people to church to hear a sermon. The New Testament pattern indicates that the church members spread God's message and as a result, the message "rang out." (See I Thessalonians 1:8.)

The following "non-biblical" methods will be examined in more detail in Section 2 but they deserve some mention here.

Jesus and His apostles never told a person to pray a "sinner's prayer."

The entire New Testament is void of a single instance in which a sinner was instructed to pray a "sinner's prayer."

Jesus and His apostles never used extra-biblical, intellectual arguments to convince people to become Christians.

Though the apostles were not ignorant of the philosophies of their day, they never used extra-biblical or philosophical arguments to intellectually convince people to become Christians.

Jesus and His apostles did not purposely invest time in developing friendships before proclaiming the gospel to people.

Jesus and the apostles proclaimed the gospel message everywhere they went and spent their time with those who seemed to receive it. There is no instance in which an apostle purposely developed a friendship with the intention of proclaiming the gospel after the relationship was better established.

Note: Most evangelical missionaries and individual Christians engage in one or more of these practices even though there is no biblical support for them.

Prepare your heart.

Before we begin talking with other people about their great need for Jesus, we must first check to see if our attitudes are right. Sometimes, it is difficult to know if any improper attitudes exist. Checking our motives for evangelizing can sometimes help us identify improper attitudes. Before we can evangelize in a way that honors Jesus, we must first discard any wrong attitudes.

Ambassadors of Christ reflect humility

All people are either ambassadors of Christ or ambassadors of Satan. There is no middle ground. Each person is either a citizen of the Kingdom of God or the kingdom of darkness. All who make up the Kingdom of God are ambassadors of Christ (II Corinthians 5:20). To represent His Kingdom, we must reflect Christ's image or the message we proclaim, even if it is biblically accurate, will be distorted by the attitudes and behavior people observe in us. To properly convey the message of the cross, we must be humble people that are moved by love for God and our fellow man.

It is essential that we first see ourselves rightly as those, who apart from Christ, deserve eternal hell. If we look down on unbelieving people as if we are superior and would never behave like them, we should examine ourselves to see if we are in the faith (II Corinthians 13:5). Hypocritical attitudes are those of an unregenerate heart. *"Why do you look at the speck of sawdust in your brother's eye and pay no attention to the plank in your own eye? How can you say to your brother, `Let me take the speck out of your eye,' when all the time there is a plank in your own eye? You hypocrite, first take the plank out of your own eye, and then you will see clearly to remove the speck from your brother's eye"* (Matthew 7:3-5). Only true believers are qualified to evangelize.

Ambassadors of Christ love as Christ loved

Besides humility, as Christ's ambassadors we must also be people that love, both in word and in deed. If we do not possess Christ-like love, we are not qualified to represent Christ to others. In fact, we are not His disciples in the first place. *"Dear children, let us not love with words or tongue but with actions and in truth. This then is how we know that we belong to the truth" (I John 3:18-19).* Jonathan Edwards said, *"If persons have the true light of heaven let into their souls, it is not a light without heat. Divine knowledge and divine love go together. A spiritual view of divine things always excites love in the soul, and draws forth the heart in love to every proper object. True discoveries of the divine character dispose us to love God as the supreme good; they unite the heart in love to Christ; they incline the soul to flow out in love to God's people, and to all mankind."* [5]

It is possible for a person to present the gospel without being a Christian. My friend's grandmother was actually going door-to-door evangelizing when she realized from the things her partner was saying that she did not know the Lord. John Wesley served as a missionary for some time before he realized that he was not a Christian. I mention this to make the point that in order to biblically evangelize, we must first possess the life of Christ. Secondly, our effectiveness at presenting Christ clearly will have a direct correlation to the degree in which His love rules our hearts. I am not suggesting that we put off the work of making disciples because we do not perfectly reflect the love of Christ.

As sinners, we will never love perfectly. But as we seek to turn sinners from the path of destruction, it is essential that they see genuine Christ-like behavior and attitudes in us. We must first possess true humility and love that reflects the image of Christ.

---

[5] Edwards, Jonathan, Charity and its Fruits, The Banner of Truth Trust, Carlisle, PA, 2000. p. 21

Discern your motives.

The Bible indicates that it is possible to evangelize with wrong motives (Philippians 1:15). An analysis of our motives may help us determine if our hearts are properly prepared for the work of evangelism. For example, what if our motivation is to merit acceptance with God? Muslims occasionally ask me why I go door-to-door proclaiming the gospel. Because of their works-based orientation to God, they assume I am doing it as a means of working my way to heaven. This is what motivates Jehovah's Witnesses. This motivation greatly dishonors God by robbing Him of the glory due His name. This motivation is that of an unregenerate heart. If a person has such a motivation, they must first cease from their dead works and come to God on His terms through the finished work of Jesus alone.

What about motivations that are not so obviously wrong? For example, what if our motive is simply to make our local church into a larger, more impressive church? Is this not prideful? Or, what if the motive is self-preservation? Several times, I have heard people say that we need to reach Muslims with the gospel in order to reduce the threat that Islam represents to our country and Christianity. I have heard other people express similar sentiment about reaching the people of the inner-city in order to save our cities from crime. By nature, these motivations indicate an attitude of superiority over the people being evangelized. "If these people were only like us, then there would be no threat of terrorism and there would be less crime in our city." Attitudes like this are akin to racism.

Christ's work has enabled Christians to be set completely free from racism and all improper attitudes and motivations for evangelism. We must first see that apart from Christ alone, we are no different than anyone we are trying to reach. Apart from Christ alone, we are no different than Hitler or any other men considered to be monsters. We may not have killed millions of people, but from God's view, there is virtually no difference between the worst monster and any other person on the face of the earth. If this is not your conviction, I recommend that you ask God to show you your sin lest you hear Jesus say on that day, *"Depart from me, I never knew you."* Remember, Jesus came to save sinners, not people who say in their hearts, *"God, I thank you that I am not like other men--robbers, evildoers, adulterers--or even like this tax collector" (Luke 18:11).*

Not only do improper motivations reflect ungodly attitudes within us, they cannot sustain a lifestyle of evangelism, especially as it is being lived out while under great trial and persecution. The more we seek to advance the Kingdom of God, the more Satan will try to destroy us. Our motivation must not come from pep talks or threats. Our motivation must come from the supernatural working of the Holy Spirit who lives within us. Our motivation must be connected directly to our view of God's glory. Only as we gaze upon Jesus and walk in His Spirit, will we be able to continue proclaiming the gospel the way God intends.

Listen to what the Apostle Paul says about these matters. *"We have this treasure in jars of clay to show that this all-surpassing power is from God and not from us. We are hard pressed on every side, but not crushed; perplexed, but not in despair; persecuted, but not abandoned; struck down, but not destroyed. We always carry around in our body the death of Jesus, so that the life of Jesus may also be revealed in our body. For we who are alive are always being given over to death for Jesus' sake, so that his life may be revealed in our mortal body. ...We do not lose heart. Though outwardly we are wasting away, yet inwardly we are being renewed day by day. For our light and momentary troubles are achieving for us an eternal glory that far outweighs them all. So we fix our eyes not on what is seen, but on what is unseen. For what is seen is temporary, but what is unseen is eternal" (II Corinthians 4:7-12, 16-18).*

We must learn to view life and evangelism from Paul's perspective. We must see that God has called us to a war that involves things and beings beyond what may be seen with the human eye. As you prepare your heart for the work of evangelism, keep fixing your eyes on things above or, like Peter, you will find yourself sinking into the water below your feet. (See Matthew 14:28-30.)

So, what should motivate us to evangelize? We should do it because **it is our delight** to see Jesus exalted as His excellencies are proclaimed. After talking with the woman at the well, Jesus' disciples brought Him food. He told them that He had food that they did not know about. Then He said that His food was to do the will of the Father. He made this statement as He was watching the people of the village coming to meet Him after hearing the woman tell them she had seen the Messiah. There have been many times that I started out discouraged going door-to-door to proclaim the gospel. After explaining the gospel to just one person, my discouragement was gone. It was as if I had eaten food for my soul. And nothing satisfies me like this type of soul food! Let us eat of this food and view it as absolutely essential for our spiritual life.

Jesus asks, "What do you seek from me?" When it comes to evangelism, have you asked yourself what you want Him to do for you. What are your prayers like? Have you ever asked Him to provide an opportunity to reach someone with the gospel? If so, that is good! If not, why have you not asked Him? Have you ever asked Him to make you into a proficient evangelist that is humble, loving and useful for the advancement of His Kingdom? If so, that is good. If not, why have you not asked Him? Jesus taught that it is an eternal blessing to be a part of this great work of His. *"I tell you, open your eyes and look at the fields! They are ripe for harvest. Even now the reaper draws his wages, even now he harvests the crop for eternal life, so that the sower and the reaper may be glad together. Thus the saying `One sows and another reaps' is true'"* (John 4:35-37).

If this is something that Jesus calls good, why not ask Him to accomplish it through you in great measure? Have you ever asked Him to use you mightily in bringing an entire multitude of people to the cross? If so, that is good. If not, why not? Would it not glorify Jesus greatly for a multitude of people to come to Him? Let us remind each other to stop looking inward and start asking God for glorious treasure- the souls of many who will praise Him forever! If we are asking these things for Jesus' sake alone, our motive for asking is good.

Count the cost

If you take the teachings of this book to heart and set yourself to do the work of evangelism, you will encounter increased opposition from Satan. The more you set yourself to do it, the greater his attack will be. Just as Jesus instructs people to count the cost of discipleship, you need to count the cost of doing this work. In reality, I consider them one in the same because I believe evangelism is merely part of true discipleship. Because the attacks will come from so many directions, I have set aside an entire section of this book to deal with this subject. As a part of your heart preparation, I strongly advise that you read Section 3 of this book, "Expect Opposition," and carefully consider the cost of setting yourself to this task.

Section 2: Doing the Work of Evangelism

-Sow the Gospel Seed
-Water the Gospel Seed.
-Harvest the Crop.

> *"Gideon ordered his men to do two things: covering up a torch in an earthen pitcher, he bade them at an appointed signal, break the pitcher and let the light shine, and then sound with the trumpet, crying, "The sword of the Lord, and of Gideon!" This is precisely what all Christians must do. First, you must shine; break the pitcher which conceals your light; throw aside the bushel which has been hiding your candle, and shine. Let your light shine before men; let your good works be such, that when men look upon you, they shall know that you have been with Jesus. Then, there must be the sound, the blowing of the trumpet. There must be active exertions for the ingathering of sinners by proclaiming Christ crucified. Take the gospel to them, carry it to their door; put it in their way; do not suffer them to escape it; **blow the trumpet right against their ears**" (Charles H. Spurgeon).*

Note: Besides the instructions provided in this section, Appendix G includes records of actual gospel conversations that might help you understand how the instructions in this Section (2) can be utilized.

Sow the gospel seed.

Before providing instruction about how to sow the gospel seed, I would like to give you a helpful suggestion that I have told numerous people. Unfortunately, this suggestion seems too simplistic to most people so it seems to fall on deaf ears most of the time. But it works. I hope you try it some time.

Are you a bit overwhelmed? Are you wondering if you will get tongue tied? Are you concerned that you might leave out some important points of the gospel? These are common fears. If you follow my suggestion, you will not have to worry about any of these things.

Follow the pattern of Jesus and the apostles by intentionally focusing primarily on sin, righteousness and judgment. If you are patient to stick to these matters and reason with people about these things until they understand their predicament, then all of the information about the good news will eventually come up automatically and in a timely way. It will spontaneously occur as the conversation progresses without you having to worry about how and when to bring it up. You don't have to rehearse any of the good news beforehand or keep it floating in your mind while you reason with the people about sin, righteousness and judgment.

Just think about this for a moment. You already know the good news. It might not always be neatly organized in your mind but it is all there. You think about Jesus and His work all the time and it makes you rejoice. Every day, you thank Him for what He has done.

Don't worry about how or when all of this information should be presented during a conversation. Here is the reason. If you patiently reason with people about their sin, God's righteousness and the coming judgment, so that the hearer begins to realize that he deserves to go to hell, you won't have to remember to tell him his need for Jesus' substitutionary sacrifice. The hearer will begin to see his need all on his own. He may even ask you, "Then who can escape the punishment of hell? Aren't we all doomed?"

Many people have asked me questions like this. If someone asked you a question like this, don't you think you would be able to answer him off the top of your head? You would not have to look at any notes. You would probably just blurt out something like this without even thinking about it, "God has made the way possible through the death of His Son Jesus!" If you said something like this, the hearer might then ask, "How is that possible?" If he asked this, you might say something like this, "He took your punishment for you!" At this point, you could probably quote John 3:16. Or, you might say something like, "The Bible promises that if any man believes that Jesus died in his place and rose from the dead, he receives remission of sins and eternal life!"

There have been a few people that have taken my advice seriously and followed my suggestion. They tried reasoning with people about sin, righteousness and judgment without worrying about how they were going to present the "good news." People who have tried this have told me afterward that the conversation was glorious and that the gospel was proclaimed in great detail. I hope you take my suggestion so you can experience this for yourself.

Having said all that, there is one thing that you might not remember to talk about if you follow my suggestion- the cost of discipleship and the subject of new life in Christ. This may happen because it is easy to get caught up in the excitement of being used by God to proclaim His excellencies. This is very important and most people forget to talk about it. The importance of discussing the cost of discipleship will be covered later in this section of the book.

Don't hide your purpose or identity as a Christian. (Be honest.)

If you tell people that you are a Christian who wants to talk with them about Jesus and the way to heaven, many of them will tell you they are not interested and walk away. Fearing this, some believers withhold their intentions hoping to warm people up before turning the conversation to the gospel. Jesus and his apostles <u>never</u> attempted to hide their purpose for initiating conversations.

It is true that if you tell people that you are a Christian who wants to talk with them about Jesus and the way to heaven, many of them will tell you they are not interested and terminate the conversation. But if you attempt to hide your purpose, the conversation may never get around to the gospel. You may end up talking with them for an hour about inconsequential things. Then, when you attempt to turn the conversation to the gospel, a person will just as likely tell you that he is not interested. He may even think you were being dishonest with him for the past hour. In reality, he would be justified for thinking this way.

I guarantee that if you attempt to evangelize people while not being forthright about your purpose, gospel proclamation will be hit and miss and you will fail to become the evangelist that God desires to make of you. In order to fulfill the great commission, you must be purposeful about proclaiming the gospel. You must make up your mind in advance to be honest with people about your purpose for talking with them. Many people will tell you they are not interested but God will arrange for some to listen in order that they hear the gospel and eventually believe.

When I evangelize, I introduce myself as a Christian. I then say that I am talking with people about the way to heaven. I then ask them if they are interested in spiritual things and the way to heaven. I do not attempt to mask my intentions. Some people tell me they are not interested but if I keep approaching people this way, it generally does not take long for me to find someone who is interested enough to listen. God is the One who is at work behind the scene to cause people to listen. Therefore, let us place our confidence in His ability to arrange for that rather than our ability to warm people up to us.

Prepare the soil by helping them see their predicament.

Usually, if you ask a man if he is a sinner, he will respond with statements like, "Of course, everyone is a sinner. Nobody is perfect." How does this answer strike you? Do you think that if you get a man to admit he is a sinner in this way that he sees himself as the Bible describes him? Let me assure you that his answer suggests just the opposite. In reality, his answer is an attempt to justify his sin. It serves as an excuse. After all, everyone is a sinner. Such a response shows that the man does not comprehend how greatly his sin offends the Holy God. This answer actually shifts some of the blame for his sin away from himself and onto God for creating him this way.

Generally, if you ask a man how a person can be made right with God, he will essentially say that as long as he tries to live a good life, God will let him into heaven. This perspective indicates a failure to comprehend the absolute righteousness of God. It makes God out to be less than perfect in His justice. It suggests that God is like a human judge who accepts plea bargains in exchange for a lighter sentence. It suggests that God will let some of those who are "guilty" of breaking His law go unpunished.

As we observed in Section 1, Jesus and the apostles always reasoned with people about sin, righteousness and judgment as THE means to prepare the heart to receive the gospel seed. They knew that, *"The man without the Spirit does not accept the things that come from the Spirit of God" (I Corinthians 2:14).* They understood that unregenerate people are spiritually blind so that:

1. They do not see themselves as God sees them.
2. They do not see God as absolutely righteous.
3. They do not see how their sin offends the holy God.

These deficiencies are common to all people of all religions and are THE reason why people do not come to Jesus for salvation. Because of this truth, the following statements are also true:

"If a man could see himself as the Holy God sees him, he would gladly believe the gospel and bow his knee to Jesus."

"Until a man gets a glimpse of himself as the Holy God sees him, he simply will not come to Christ."

We must try to help people see themselves and God rightly so they can be saved. To do this, we must explain what the Bible says about God's absolute righteousness and what it says about their wretched condition as rebels against God.

While it is always helpful to understand the culture of the person with whom we are speaking, the message itself never changes. What do the following people all have in common?

The Jew

The Muslim

The polytheistic Hindu

The Buddhist

The animist from China

The atheist

The Jehovah's Witness

These people are all sinners in the hands of an angry God. It makes no difference whether or not they believe that God exists, or that there is more than one God or that the Bible is the Word of God or that Jesus is God the Son. Our message remains the same. We must first try to help them see themselves and God rightly so that they begin to realize that in reality, God views them as His enemies who rightly deserve the sentence of eternal hell.

When Jesus spoke with the woman at the well and when Paul addressed the people at Athens, they opened their conversations by saying things calculated to get the attention of their hearers. They did not immediately begin hammering the people about their sin. But before they even began to speak, they had full intentions of addressing issues like sin, righteousness and judgment. Their opening attention-getting statements were merely the means they used to direct the conversation to the weightier matters intended to cut to the heart. This is the pattern we see in discussions initiated by Jesus and His apostles.

If an atheist insists that there is no God, he does it to his own condemnation. We have no power to make him believe "from the heart" that God exists. If a Muslim refuses to listen, claiming that the Bible cannot be trusted, he does so to his own condemnation. We have no power to make him believe "from the heart" that the Bible is God's Word. If a Jehovah's Witness insists that Jesus is something less than God, he does so to his own condemnation. We have no power to make him believe "from the heart" that Jesus is Lord.

Though it may be possible to convince some people of truth intellectually, it is impossible to make them believe it "from their heart." Only God can do this. Our job is to humbly speak the truth of the full gospel with a heart of love for God as Jesus and His disciples spoke it. But it is also our job to seek God's power to do so and to learn how to do it more effectively. He is able to make us skillful surgeons that know how to specifically apply the scalpel of truth in such a way that it produces true conviction. Even if the hearer refuses to believe at that moment, the seed has opportunity to take root in soil that is properly prepared.

I have presented the gospel in this way to thousands of people that had actually heard it before I explained it to them. But because I patiently and lovingly first helped them to understand that, according to the Bible, they are considered wicked in God's sight and fully deserving of hell, many of them told me that the message they were hearing from me was new to them, even though they had already heard it. Because they had not understood the Bible's teaching about sin, righteousness and judgment to come, the gospel did not register in their minds and it did not leave an impression on their hearts. The connection between their sin and the cross did not take place until they first heard what the Bible says about their condition before God. Many have heard the phrase, "Jesus died for our sins." Now, for the first time, many people with whom I have spoken finally understood the connection between their sin and the need for Jesus' sacrificial death.

Steer conversations down the biblical path!

Since it is our first goal to help the hearer see his predicament, we need to steer the conversation accordingly. In order to build a foundation for a discussion that will accomplish this, first ascertain what the hearer believes about the way to heaven. This may be as simple as asking him to tell you how a person can gain heaven. You could ask, "Why should God let you or me into heaven?" Virtually every person you meet will essentially tell you that in order to get to heaven, a man must earn acceptance with God by doing good works. Make it your first goal to get the person to vocalize this in his own words. Once he does, the foundation is laid for a potentially fruitful discussion. At this point, you might say, "According to the Bible, it is impossible to get to heaven that way." You can then begin to teach him what the Bible says about his sinfulness, God's righteousness and the judgment to come. As a result, he will realize that according to the Bible, he cannot earn his way to heaven and that he stands condemned.

Know the milestones of an Effective Gospel Discussion

You can begin a gospel conversation talking about perhaps anything imaginable. The conversation is dynamic so it will have a tendency to go in various directions. Lack of time might prevent you from fully presenting the gospel during the conversation. But if you achieve the following basic milestones, you will most likely end up presenting the entire gospel so that the unbeliever comprehends it at least with his mind. I recommend that you let these milestones guide you through every gospel conversation.

Milestone 1: Get the unbeliever to tell you what he believes is "the way to heaven."[6]

This milestone can happen near the beginning of a discussion and it serves as THE foundation for the rest of the conversation.

Milestone 2: Get the unbeliever to either wonder or actually say out loud, "Well, what hope is there for anyone?...you seem to be saying that everyone is doomed to go to hell forever."

Achieving this milestone may take up to an hour or two in some cases. The only way to achieve this milestone is to talk about God's absolute righteousness and man's absolute sinfulness. It requires patience to do this properly. If you gloss over this without the unbeliever coming to this conclusion in his mind, he will not properly see the connection to the cross. Jesus' death will remain unimportant to him. So keep talking about sin, righteousness and judgment until he begins to wonder, "What hope is there for anyone?"

---

[6] If the person does not believe there is a God, you can still get him to tell you what he thinks "Christians" believe is the way to heaven.

Milestone 3: Help him see how Jesus made it possible for him to be reconciled to God through His substitutionary death.

Milestone 4: Help him count the cost of becoming a disciple of Jesus. (Explain what happens when God regenerates a person. Tell him how He did this for you.)

If you are committed to help people see their true condition and would like to improve your ability to do so, I strongly urge you to acquaint yourself with "God's Redemption Message" study that you can download free from the **Stones Cry Out web site.**[7] This material has proven itself extremely useful in conveying what the Bible says about God's righteousness, their sinfulness, and the salvation that is available to them through Jesus' work on the cross. Even though most unbelievers will not be willing to go through all of this material with you, I recommend that you still review the material yourself and make note of Bible verses that you would like to incorporate into your evangelism arsenal. Perhaps you should highlight them in your Bible or write down the references in the front of your Bible. If you have your Bible with you during a subsequent conversation, you can stress special points by looking up an appropriate verse and then asking the person to read it out loud. This can help them learn what the Bible teaches about sin, righteousness and judgment.

---

[7] The Stones Cry Out web site is found at **www.StonesCryOut.INFO**. Go to the Free Evangelism Tools page selected from the top of the home page.

Fulfil your role as one of God's "prophets."

> *"'Before I formed you in the womb I knew you, before you were born I set you apart; I appointed you as a prophet to the nations.' 'Ah, Sovereign LORD,' I said, 'I do not know how to speak; I am only a child.' But the LORD said to me, 'Do not say, `I am only a child.' You must go to everyone I send you to and say whatever I command you. Do not be afraid of them, for I am with you and will rescue you,' declares the LORD. Then the LORD reached out His hand and touched my mouth and said to me, 'Now, I have put my words in your mouth. See, today I appoint you over nations and kingdoms to uproot and tear down, to destroy and overthrow, to build and to plant....Get yourself ready! Stand up and say to them whatever I command you. Do not be terrified by them, or I will terrify you before them'" (Jeremiah 1:5-10,17).*

While we are not all apostles, prophets, evangelists or pastors in the sense that Paul meant in Ephesians 4:11, we are all ambassadors that represent Christ. In the same way that Jeremiah was called to speak forth God's truth, we must all learn to view ourselves as God's prophets who have been given the solemn task of speaking forth the truth that is offensive and foolish to the natural man. If we fail to speak forth the truth about the predicament of the unbeliever in such a way that causes an impact, our message will have the opposite effect upon the hearer. He will be lulled to sleep and be further convinced that he has no reason to be alarmed about his condition.

Concerning the false prophets of his day, Jeremiah said, *"They have lied about the LORD; they said, "He will do nothing! No harm will come to us; we will never see sword or famine" (Jeremiah 5:12).* If we avoid talking about an unbeliever's sin, God's righteousness and the judgment to come, he will be made to think that everything is okay and there is nothing to be troubled about. Though unintentional, we might effectively be giving a message of peace when judgment is looming over the head of the hearer. God does not want the hearer to think that everything is peaceful between God and him. Let the seriousness of His pronouncement against the false prophets make us careful to warn people about their predicament.

"Then the LORD said to me, 'The prophets are prophesying lies in my name. I have not sent them or appointed them or spoken to them. They are prophesying to you false visions, divinations, idolatries and the delusions of their own minds. Therefore, this is what the LORD says about the prophets who are prophesying in my name: I did not send them, yet they are saying, 'No sword or famine will touch this land.' Those same prophets will perish by sword and famine. And the people they are prophesying to will be thrown out into the streets of Jerusalem because of the famine and sword. There will be no one to bury them or their wives, their sons or their daughters. I will pour out on them the calamity they deserve'" (Jeremiah 14:14-16)._

Too many people think of Jesus only as the gentle baby in the manger. It is our responsibility to warn them that He is the Almighty Judge that will soon mete out judgment. *"Out of his mouth comes a sharp sword with which to strike down the nations. He will rule them with an iron scepter.* **He treads the winepress of the fury of the wrath of God Almighty"** *(Revelation 19:15).* It would be unloving to withhold or gloss over the truth so that the unbeliever goes away thinking that he does not have to be concerned about the wrath of God.

Help the hearer understand the cost of discipleship.

Evangelism includes the task of making the cost of discipleship known to an unbeliever. Discussing the cost of true discipleship is like digging into the soil so that the gospel seed has a place to take root. But the timing of this task depends on God's leading. Unless a person is at least beginning to understand that he deserves condemnation and that the remedy may be found only in Christ, it may not be the time to discuss the cost of true discipleship. But as progress is being made beyond mental comprehension and into the area of the heart, we must tell him that he must lose his life unto Christ in order to find it. I often quote Jesus, *"Whoever does not bear his cross and come after Me **cannot be My disciple**" (Luke 14:27).*

He must be made to understand that once a man believes from the heart, the life he has been living will no longer be the same. God will begin to make him hate the things he has loved and love the things that God loves. Instead of being swept along by fleshly desires, as a believer, he will find himself swimming upstream against the current of sinful cravings. The hearer must be told that unless he is willing to lose the life he currently loves for Christ's sake and suffer for Him, he is not worthy to be called His disciple.

By making the cost known to him, he will be forced to further engage the gospel with his heart, not just his mind. We know that a person cannot be saved until the heart is brought to bear on these matters because it is with the heart that man believes. *"For it is with your heart that you believe and are justified, and it is with your mouth that you confess and are saved" (Romans 10:10).* Therefore, we should bring up the cost of discipleship when it appears that the person is beginning to comprehend his predicament and is beginning to appreciate the good news of Jesus' sacrificial death.

Observe the reaction to evaluate progress.

One time, after talking with a Muslim man for several minutes about sin, righteousness and judgment, I summed up by stating that, due to these things, everyone on earth deserves to go to hell forever. The man scowled and said, "That's stupid!" Then he turned and said, "That's stupid," "That's stupid," repeatedly, as he walked away. Now this may seem like a failed attempt to evangelize but at least this man understood this part of the message, even though he did not accept it that moment. I should also mention that I cannot recall another conversation that ended that way.

In your conversations, look for some sort of reaction to the message. If you get no reaction, then either you have not made the truth about the unbeliever's predicament clear or he simply has not been listening. Since some people are hard to read, it sometimes helps to interject questions like, "Have you ever heard this before?" or "Does this news sound like good news or bad news?" If the hearer does not seem to be reacting, he probably has not yet comprehended the gravity of his condition before God.

People are amazingly proficient at selectively tuning out things they do not want to hear. Since most people think they already have the answers to life, they tend to listen in a way that filters the information through their system of looking at things. I have had conversations with some people during which I clearly told them that they stood condemned before God and were headed for hell. Yet, they just smiled politely. In many such cases, I asked questions or made statements that might help me determine if the person understood what I was saying. Often, it was clear that they just were not getting it.

After lengthy discussions about sin, righteousness, judgment and the need for a substitutionary sacrifice, I have asked people how a person can be made acceptable to God only to have them say, "By doing good works." Such a response indicates that they still do not understand their predicament. It was if they had not heard anything I had said to them. I have found that it usually takes several minutes and sometimes hours of reasoning with people about sin, righteousness and judgment before they really begin to sense their condition. You need to get accustomed to repeatedly steering conversations back to the need for salvation to help people comprehend their predicament.

Just as Jesus often did, we should not hesitate to bring up specific sins under the magnifying glass of the law. Go through the commandments with them to show that they have broken them. It is often necessary to make true statements that are designed to get their attention such as, "The Bible says that all of us, including you and me, deserve to go to hell forever." Or, "Did you know that God's wrath is resting on all who do not follow Jesus?" I am not suggesting we do this in a mean-spirited fashion. We must humbly speak to the listener in a sincere and loving manner so that he understands that we see ourselves as wretched sinners as well. But we must not dodge the important issues of sin, righteousness and judgment to come.

Scripture contains many examples of God's people being blunt about these matters: Paul with Felix (Acts 24:24-25), John the Baptist with Herod (Matthew 14:3-5), Peter with Simon the sorcerer (Acts 8:18-24) and Paul with the magician (Acts 13:9-11). If we faithfully stick to these principles, some conversations might be cut short because the listener will not like what he is hearing. We should not be troubled that we did not get a chance to explain the "good news." It is great when we get to do so but the fact that the listener reacted so negatively may be a very good sign that we struck a nerve that needed to be struck. We must keep in mind that God is fully capable of bringing someone else into his life to continue the discourse. Our goal should be to sow seeds of gospel truth in each conversation and pray that God sends others to water the seed. Remember, God alone gives the increase.

Consider the culture but never alter the message!

Besides learning how to evangelize after the pattern of Jesus and His apostles, I also suggest that you consider the culture of the people you hope to evangelize. Paul said, *"Though I am free and belong to no man, I make myself a slave to everyone, to win as many as possible. To the Jews I became like a Jew, to win the Jews. To those under the law I became like one under the law (though I myself am not under the law), so as to win those under the law. To those not having the law I became like one not having the law (though I am not free from God's law but am under Christ's law), so as to win those not having the law. To the weak I became weak, to win the weak. I have become all things to all men so that by all possible means I might save some. I do all this for the sake of the gospel, that I may share in its blessings"* (I Corinthians 9:19-23). It is wise to consider that there are likely some things about the culture that are good to know if your goal is to reach some for Christ. For example, in many Middle-Eastern cultures, it is considered an insult if you show someone the bottom of your shoe. If you are trying to reach people in such cultures, it is helpful to know this so that you can avoid offending someone needlessly.

While it is wise to learn about the culture in order to avoid needless offenses, we must <u>never alter the message of the gospel in our attempts to reach people!</u>

Even if we or an angel from heaven should preach a gospel other than the one we preached to you, let him be eternally condemned! As we have already said, so now I say again: If anybody is preaching to you a gospel other than what you accepted, let him be eternally condemned! (Galatians 1:8-9)

Since the Apostle Paul pronounced such a curse against anyone preaching a different gospel, all Christians do well to examine the gospel they preach and be extremely careful to correct anything deficient in the message they proclaim. The redemption message must never change! There are many people living in the twenty-first century that have erroneously suggested that before we reach out to people, we must study their culture in order to develop a message that will not offend them. For example, to be less offensive, many missionaries now use the Qur'an instead of the Bible to evangelize Muslims. I hope you recognize, especially in light of the Apostle Paul's warning, that such a practice is a dangerous violation of God's will. Just remember, God's message of redemption must not be altered!

Do not rely on extra-biblical, intellectual arguments.[8]

"It is impossible to convince a man to believe by simply addressing all of his intellectual objections" (Tom Bear).

During the past century, the evangelical church has drifted from a reliance on the gospel itself and has increased its dependence on the use of extra-biblical, intellectual arguments in order to "convince people to become Christians." When I first came to Christ in the late 1970's, I enjoyed reading a book by Paul Little entitled, "How to Give Away Your Faith." This book, like many similar books, presents logical arguments that support various Christian beliefs. Examples of these beliefs include the infallibility of the Bible, the existence of God and the deity of Christ. In his book, Paul Little taught that we should use these arguments to address intellectual objections to the gospel message. I learned some of these and used them at times when discussing the gospel with unbelievers. One of my favorites states that Jesus could only be one of the following:

-the Son of God
-a liar
-a lunatic
-a legend

---

[8] In this book, "extra-biblical arguments" are defined as arguments not contained in the Bible that are designed to provide intellectual reasons that support various Christian beliefs. Many people call these intellectual arguments "apologetics." Examples of these beliefs include the infallibility of the Bible, the existence of God, the deity of Christ, etc. Such beliefs are taught by the Bible but some people use intellectual arguments based upon logic in an attempt to prove to people that these things are true. Since the arguments themselves are not contained in the Bible, I classify them as "extra-biblical."

This argument states that there can be no other logical possibility. For example, He could not have merely been a good man because a good man does not claim to be the Son of God if he is just a man. If He were merely a man, then stating such a claim would make him either a lunatic or a liar. Either way, He would not qualify as a good man.

While I enjoy reading such logical arguments and would never discourage others from doing the same, I believe that dependence on them in evangelistic outreach is unfounded, biblically speaking. In fact, Paul would say that to do so makes the cross "empty of its power" (see I Corinthians 1:17). Please consider some observations from the Bible and ask yourself if perhaps you might be wrongly relying on the use of extra-biblical, intellectual arguments in order to "convince people to become Christians."

As we already observed from Luke's testimony in Acts, Paul "reasoned" with his hearers. Please understand that I am not suggesting that we abandon the biblical practice of reasoning with people. As you study the Bible, ask yourself, "What did the Apostle Paul, Jesus and the other disciples reason with their hearers about?" Was their reasoning designed to address intellectual objections raised by the hearer? Were they debating the existence of God? Were they debating the authenticity of the Scripture? Were they using extra-biblical, intellectual arguments to prove that Jesus was God come in the flesh? By examining the biblical record, you will see that they were not doing any of these things.

Some have suggested that Paul used extra-biblical arguments in his short sermon at Athens (Acts 17). I suggest that upon closer investigation, you will see that he merely used extra-biblical data to gain the attention of his hearers, not debate or convince them. Once he had their attention, Paul immediately shifted the attention to gospel truth that was aimed at the heart, not the intellect. It is noteworthy that he did not debate the existence of the One True and Living God with the polytheists in the crowd. He merely stated as fact that He is the Creator and that, as His creatures, all people are accountable to Him and should therefore **REPENT**. Then he said that God has appointed a man (Jesus) to **judge the world in righteousness** and proved it by **raising Him from the dead.** (Acts 17:22-31.)

Paul did not rely on intellectual arguments in his preaching. He relied on the biblical truth calculated to impact the heart. This is in keeping with his testimony, *"My message and my preaching were not with wise and persuasive words, but with a demonstration of the Spirit's power, so that your faith might not rest on men's wisdom, but on God's power" (I Corinthians 2:4-5).* Rather than depend on carefully crafted arguments to persuade men intellectually, he stuck with the gospel itself that he referred to as, *"the power of God unto salvation to all who believe" (Romans 1:16).* He obviously knew that many people would think of him as an intellectual fool for preaching the gospel because he also said, *"The message of the cross is foolishness to those who are perishing, but to us who are being saved it is the power of God" (I Corinthians 1:18).*

Paul was an intellectual giant in his day. Yet, when we study the book of Acts and Paul's epistles, we see that Paul resisted the use of his superior knowledge to debate with people merely on an intellectual level. Rather, he reasoned with people about the same types of things that Jesus reasoned with them about. The Bible says that Paul reasoned with people "from the scriptures" (Acts 17:2). I cannot find any examples of Paul relying on extra-biblical, intellectual arguments designed to "convince people to become Christians."

Why do so many Christians rely so much on the use of extra-biblical, intellectual arguments in their evangelistic outreach? Perhaps they falsely think that if only they can convince people that their intellectual objections are unfounded, nothing will prevent them from making a decision to start following Christ.

I have heard some people use I Peter 3:15 to support the use of extra-biblical, intellectual arguments in evangelistic outreach. *"But in your hearts set apart Christ as Lord. Always be prepared to give an answer to everyone who asks you to give the reason for the hope that you have."* The word "answer" is used to translate the Greek word "apologia." In this verse, Peter refers to that which produces hope in us. What is it that produces hope in the believer? Is it a series of intellectual arguments that justify our position?

Be Ready to Give an Answer.

It is clear that Peter instructed Christians to be ready always to give an answer to every man that asks him the reason of the hope that is in him. Unfortunately, many Christians misunderstand what type of answer Peter had in mind and how it should be provided. Most Christians think that if they are to fulfill Peter's instructions, they must learn various intellectual arguments aimed at convincing people that God exists, or that Jesus rose from the dead, or that the Bible is the infallible Word of God, or other such things. This is not at all what Peter had in mind. Let us consider I Peter 3:15 along with other scriptures to determine how we should understand him properly.

First, it should be noted that in order to fulfill this instruction, we must first "sanctify the Lord God in our heart." This is the essential prerequisite and in fact the only way we can "be ready" to give an answer. Notice Peter does not say, "First, learn whatever intellectual arguments necessary so that you will be ready to give an answer." No, he instructs us to do something spiritual- "Sanctify the Lord God in your heart." It is not an intellectual preparing but a spiritual preparing that is specified by the phrase "sanctify the Lord Jesus in your heart." The New American Standard Bible translates it, *"Sanctify Christ as Lord in your hearts, always being ready to make a defense."* This indicates a cause and effect relationship. If we do not first "sanctify Christ as Lord in our heart," then we simply won't be ready to give an answer. But if we do sanctify Christ as Lord in our heart, we will be ready to give an answer.

So what does it mean to sanctify Christ as Lord in our heart? I suggest it can also be stated, *"I beseech you therefore, brethren, by the mercies of God, that you present your bodies a living sacrifice, holy, acceptable to God, which is your reasonable service. And do not be conformed to this world, but be transformed by the renewing of your mind, that you may prove what is that good and acceptable and perfect will of God"* (Romans 12:1-2). It means total surrender with nothing held back. After all, Jesus is Lord, the ruler and He owns me. I don't have a right to direct my life because it is now His. I am bought with the price of Jesus' blood. Unless and until this surrender is a reality in the life of a Christian, he will not experience what it means to walk in the Spirit. If not fully surrendered, his spiritual experience with Christ will be dysfunctional. In this condition, he will not be spiritually prepared to give an answer about the hope that is within him. In fact, that hope will be dim because the experience of Jesus living in him will be difficult to discern by him.

The true Christian life requires total surrender with nothing held back. (*"Whoever seeks to save his life will lose it, and whoever loses his life will preserve it"* Luke 17:33.) In this condition, the Spirit has free reign and the Christian is empowered by God's grace to walk in the Spirit and fulfill His good pleasure. As he walks in the Spirit, he experiences the reality of Jesus living in him. In this condition, he experiences the hope of eternal life. *"Christ in you, the hope of glory"* (Colossians 1:27). His hope is not generated from head knowledge. A man can know all the creeds and intellectually agree with all the doctrines of the Christian faith and yet not possess hope. Hope comes only when a man's <u>experience</u> is in harmony with his doctrine. Without his experience being in complete harmony with his doctrine, he really cannot possess hope and therefore cannot fulfill Peter's instruction. This is why Peter begins by saying, "Sanctify Christ as Lord in your hearts."

With all these things in mind, let us now consider the nature of the answer we are to give for the hope that is in us. Before doing so, let me address a common misconception relating to the Greek word "apologia" that Peter used when he said "be ready to give an <u>answer</u>." The Greek word apologia can mean "a defense" or "an answer." The KJV translates it *answer* while the NASB translates it *defense*. Many Christians mistakenly think that I Peter 3:15 teaches we must be ready to effectively debate those who argue against the tenants of the Christian faith. In other words, we should be ready to prove that what we believe is intellectually reasonable and logical. This is not what Peter is saying. He says, "Be ready always to give an answer to anyone who asks you <u>a reason for the hope that is in you</u>." Our answer, or "defense," is in response to someone who asks us a reason for the hope that is in us. Our answer is <u>NOT</u> in response to the skeptic who asks, "Why do you believe such an absurd thing?" Peter is indicating that the question being asked is coming from a person who is <u>sincerely wondering</u> <u>why we have **hope**.</u>

It MUST be noted that a major theme in Peter's first epistle is the **suffering** that Christians endure because they follow Jesus. The recipients of his letter were often threatened with death and had undergone much persecution. As the unbelievers observed the Christians suffering, they took notice that they seemed to have hope in spite of all the mistreatment and suffering. This undoubtedly caused some to ask Christians the reason for their hope. It didn't make sense to them that they willingly endured so much suffering. Why did they have hope?

What is the basis for a Christian's hope? Is it because there is strong evidence that God exists? Is it because there is strong evidence that Jesus rose from the dead? Is it because there is strong evidence that the Bible is the authoritative Word of God that He has faithfully preserved? I believe that there is strong evidence for all these things but the evidence, though intellectually convincing, **cannot produce hope**! If a man's hope is based solely on such evidence, then his hope has no depth and if faced with the threat of severe persecution and death, it will evaporate. The hope that Peter is talking about is the sure promise of God itself (the Gospel) and the reality of it being lived out in us (*Christ in you, the hope of glory.*)

Therefore, if a Christian stoops to debating by using intellectual arguments that he believes prove things like the existence of God, Jesus' resurrection from the dead, etc., he is failing to fulfill Peter's instructions in I Peter 3:15. Instead of doing this, he should proclaim the Gospel itself for this is the objective reason for the hope that is in him. He can also testify about the reality of Jesus living in him which is evidenced by a completely changed life. These things answer anyone who sincerely asks a reason for the hope that is in the Christian.

When we understand this properly, then we realize why there is no record in the New Testament of any Christian leaders making intellectual arguments in order to prove that God exists, or that Jesus rose from the dead, or that the Bible is the infallible Word of God, or other such things. On the contrary, we see an excellent example of how Paul fulfilled Peter's instruction when we read the book of Romans. This is a letter he wrote to people he had not met. In it, he gave a very detailed answer for the hope that was in him. Being a lawyer, he did so in such a way that it truly qualifies as "a defense" for the hope that was within him. He did not give evidence for the existence of God. He merely stated it. He did not sight evidence that Jesus rose from the dead. He merely stated it. He did not give evidence that the Bible is the authoritative Word of God, he merely quoted it as if it is indeed God's Word. He did not try to prove that Jesus was God incarnate. He simply proclaimed it.

The book of Romans contains the message Paul proclaimed wherever he went. Its content is in harmony with Paul's testimony from his first epistle to the Corinthians.

"Christ did not send me to baptize, but to preach the gospel, not with wisdom of words, lest the cross of Christ should be made of no effect" (I Corinthians 1:17).

"My speech and my preaching were <u>not with persuasive words of human</u> <u>wisdom</u>, but in demonstration of the Spirit and of power, that your faith should not be in the wisdom of men but in the power of God" (I Corinthians 2:4-5).

Paul did not debate the Gospel. Rather, he proclaimed it. As he did in his epistle to the Romans, Paul publicly reasoned with people about the same things hoping they would hear and believe. Whenever they refused to receive it, he would not debate with them. Rather, he warned them and then left them and went to find other people who would hear and believe. Below is just one example Luke gives in Acts of Paul doing this. There are several others.

But when the Jews saw the crowds, they were filled with jealousy and began contradicting the things spoken by Paul, and were blaspheming. Paul and Barnabas spoke out boldly and said, "It was necessary that the word of God be spoken to you first; since you repudiate it and judge yourselves unworthy of eternal life, behold, we are turning to the Gentiles" (Acts 13:45-46 NASB).

Luke records how Paul ministered the Gospel and thus fulfilled Peter's instruction.

And according to Paul's custom, he went to them, and for three Sabbaths reasoned with them from the Scriptures, explaining and giving evidence that the Christ had to suffer and rise again from the dead, and saying, "This Jesus whom I am proclaiming to you is the Christ" (Acts 17:2-3 NASB).

Paul was fulfilling Peter's instruction. He was giving an answer (making a defense) for the hope that was in him. The hearers in this case included some Jews and also some Gentiles that had been exposed to the Jewish Scriptures. The recipients already believed in the existence of God and believed the Scriptures were God's authoritative Word. But many of them did not believe that Jesus was the Messiah or that He rose from the dead. So, Paul reasoned with them <u>FROM THE SCRIPTURES</u> giving evidence that the Christ had to suffer (as a substitute sacrifice for sins) and rise from the dead. To make his case, he did not merely read passages like Isaiah 53 and Psalm 22. He reasoned with them from the Scriptures to demonstrate WHY the Christ had to suffer. This is exactly what Paul does in Romans chapters 1 – 3.

The reason why the Christ had to suffer is that sinful man is alienated from the Holy God, condemned and headed for eternal punishment. God, being perfectly righteous cannot let the guilty go unpunished. The sin had to be punished. If people come to the judgment with their sins, God has no choice but to send them to hell forever because He cannot simply excuse sin. Sinful man can do nothing to make himself acceptable to God. But God provided a way of salvation by sending His own Son to take the punishment we deserve. This is why the Christ had to suffer. There could be no other way of salvation. Since Jesus did come and complete His work, there is salvation and therefore hope that is based upon the sure promise of God. Paul's message gives the hearer the solid reason for the hope within him.

Seeing that there is no biblical record of leaders trying to convince people that God exists, or that Jesus rose from the dead, or that the Bible is the infallible Word of God, or other such things, why do Christians insist we need to do it? It seems as if they do not believe as fully as Paul believed that THE GOSPEL is the power of God unto salvation. Otherwise, instead of trying to prove things like the existence of God, that Jesus rose from the dead, the integrity of the Bible, they would concentrate of proclaiming the Gospel which is THE MEANS God has specified to save people.

Maybe the problem is that they do not consistently engage in evangelism. Then, when they do engage in it, they typically find themselves talking with a skeptic. Rather than just warn the skeptic and walk away as Paul did, they sense a responsibility to continue the dialog since they don't often find themselves engaged in evangelism. Perhaps if they engaged in it much more, they would realize that instead of talking with the skeptics, it is far more productive to warn and leave them and then seek out those whom God has prepared to hear the Gospel and concentrate on proclaiming the Gospel to them.

Maybe the reason is a defective theology. For example, many Christians hold to an Arminian theology that teaches unregenerate man has the power within himself to seek God. Since in their minds, man has this power, it behooves the evangelist to do everything in his power to intellectually convince the unregenerate man to seek God by offering all sorts of logical evidence for things like the existence of God, the integrity of the scripture and Jesus' resurrection from the dead. They think that if the unregenerate man can be convinced of things like this, then he will more likely decide to become a Christian.

Someone might ask, "Why am I making such a big fuss over all this anyway? Does it matter that much if a Christian makes efforts to provide historical, logical or scientific evidence for things like the existence of God, etc?" I make a fuss over this because I think the Apostle Paul would make a fuss over it. He said to the Corinthians:

"My speech and my preaching were <u>not with persuasive words of human wisdom,</u> but in demonstration of the Spirit and of power, that your faith should not be in the wisdom of men but in the power of God" (I Corinthians 2:4-5).

Paul also thought that if he resorted to using "wisdom of words," the cross of Christ would be made of no effect. (See I Corinthians 1:17.) I have watched public debates between Christian apologists and leaders of other religions or atheists. Generally, those who attend are already set in their thinking. Spectators from both sides usually go away thinking their side won the debate. The worst thing is that many go away thinking that two different views were presented and each view had some merit. This is not how the Gospel should be represented. It is not just another possible viewpoint. It is <u>the only way</u> of salvation and no other view should be given any credence whatsoever. Engaging in such a debate automatically gives the opposing view some credence. As a result, the cross of Jesus is made to appear less than what it is. It is emptied of its power in the eyes of many who watched. THE GOSPEL IS NOT TO BE DEBATED! The Apostle Paul refused to do so and so should we. It is the Holy Gospel of Jesus Christ. Let us represent it as if it is truly the only way of salvation purchased by the precious blood of Jesus.

Let us do as Peter instructed us in I Peter 3:15 but let us do so in accordance with the biblical pattern and with the full authority given us by Christ. Let us therefore sanctify Christ as Lord in our hearts so there is nothing held back whatsoever.

Unless we sanctify Christ as Lord in our hearts, our hope will be dim. To unbelievers, we will appear like everyone else, living our lives as if there is no God and no future hope. But if we sanctify Christ as Lord in our hearts, the Gospel will continually be in our hearts and minds and unbelievers that come in contact with us will notice something different about us. Our hope will be evident. Unbelievers will occasionally ask us a reason for the hope that is in us. When they do, we will have the privilege of proclaiming the same glorious truths that Paul recorded for us in the book of Romans.

Let us preach the gospel, not debate it.

Please understand that I am not saying that it is wrong to learn apologetic arguments. In fact, I would recommend that Christians read books that contain them. I think that such arguments have their basis in logic and as such can be employed in our meditations about God, Jesus and His wonderful Word to us. Yet, I think that many Christians have fallen into the habit of wrongly relying on the use of these extra-biblical, intellectual arguments as if they form a biblical basis for evangelistic outreach. It is impossible to convince a man to believe by simply addressing all of his intellectual objections.

The key element of evangelizing the lost is not the use of extra-biblical, intellectual arguments but rather, the communication of the gospel in such a way that the listener gains a mental understanding of its relevance so that it leaves an impression on his heart. As long as the listener understands our language, this can be accomplished regardless of his background, because all people have the same need! They are all sinners that have a false comprehension of their condition before God. If the listener gains a mental comprehension of the gospel in such a way that his heart is impacted, God is then able to regenerate him whenever He decides because the gospel is the supernatural seed of God. *"Faith comes by hearing and hearing by the word of God" (Romans 10:17).* When we reason with people, let us use the biblical record as the foundation to demonstrate how God has poured out His mercy by coming to earth as a blood sacrifice who would bear the punishment people deserve in such a way that His righteous demands were fully satisfied.

Avoid arguing with unbelievers about their pet points.

Normally, unbelievers do not want to talk about the truth. They usually try to avoid it. *"Everyone who does evil hates the light, and will not come into the light for fear that his deeds will be exposed" (John 3:20).* If unbelievers don't want to be entirely rude by slamming the door in our faces, they will try and deflect the discussion away from the gospel by citing their own talking points. The woman at the well did this during her conversation with Jesus when she tried to suggest that "she had her religion." She was a Samaritan and Jesus was speaking from the standpoint of a Jew. To deflect the argument, she tried to imply that since she was not a Jew, the things Jesus was saying did not apply to her. Rather than debate her, Jesus simply quoted truth from the Scripture as the final word. Muslims will try to deflect the conversation by saying they don't believe Jesus died or that the Bible cannot be trusted. It does not matter what they believe intellectually. Our approach should be the same as that of Jesus and His apostles. We should point them right back to the truth, fully believing in our hearts that the Bible is God's Word and that Jesus did indeed die because man is guilty and has no way of paying the price required for all his sin.

Because we are fully convinced of these things, we don't have to feel as if it is our job to defend our position. Rather, we can come right back to the subjects that they don't want to face: their sin, God's righteousness and their just condemnation. After they understand what the Bible says about their predicament, we can reason with them about gospel truth. For example, we can get them to mentally agree that if the Almighty God did indeed come to earth in order to sacrificially die in their place, such an act would be a powerful demonstration of His love for them personally. So, even if they refuse to believe the truth, we can reason with them about it in order to convey gospel truth.

Discern when to stop talking.

Jesus said, *"If anyone will not welcome you or listen to your words, shake the dust off your feet when you leave that home or town" (Matthew 10:14).* In most major cities, there is not enough dust swirling around to collect on the streets. Unless we are in a remote rural area, we won't have dust on our feet. So, do we simply discard Jesus' instruction to "shake the dust off our feet" when we encounter those who will not listen to our message? Is there anything in His instruction that applies to us today? I believe that there <u>are</u> times when we must withhold the gospel.

The Bible says that we are to *"answer a fool according to his folly" (Proverbs 26:5).* There is a prerequisite to the application of this instruction. It assumes that we ourselves are not "fools." It is possible for us to act as a fool and this is done whenever we are wise in our own eyes. In fact, if we are wise in our own eyes, the fool is better off than us (Proverbs 26:12). The Bible teaches that we must use discretion when talking with people and sometimes this requires us to avoid answering foolish objections or questions or even cease talking completely. But our attitude must be right in the first place. If we are wise in our own eyes, then we cannot apply the principle taught by Proverbs 26:5 and Matthew 10:14 because to do so, we would be playing the hypocrite.

When a man that is wise in his own eyes preaches the gospel, its beauty is marred and its glory tarnished. We must not give cause to the wicked to speak ill of the Name. But if we are walking in the Spirit, we will be enjoying clear eyesight that allows us to see ourselves, others and God properly. Only in this condition, with all planks removed, will we be able to see clearly enough to remove the speck from our friend's eye (Matthew 7:5). It is only then   that we are wise enough to follow the teaching of the next verse, *"Do not cast your pearls before swine"(Matthew 7:6).* Perhaps the Holy Spirit has not yet prepared this ground.

If we are going door-to-door and a person slams the door in our faces before we even get an opportunity to tell him our purpose for being there, do we "shake the dust off our feet" in a figurative sense? The feeling of personal rejection might incline us to do so, but that is not sufficient reason to "shake the dust off our feet." For all we know, he might have thought we were sales people. The story of Phinehas sheds some light on this subject.

"Moses said to Israel's judges, "Each of you must put to death those of your men who have joined in worshiping the Baal of Peor." Then an Israelite man brought to his family a Midianite woman right before the eyes of Moses and the whole assembly of Israel while they were weeping at the entrance to the Tent of Meeting. When Phinehas son of Eleazar, the son of Aaron, the priest, saw this, he left the assembly, took a spear in his hand and followed the Israelite into the tent. He drove the spear through both of them--through the Israelite and into the woman's body. Then the plague against the Israelites was stopped; but those who died in the plague numbered 24,000. The LORD said to Moses, "Phinehas son of Eleazar, the son of Aaron, the priest, has turned my anger away from the Israelites; for he was as zealous as I am for my honor among them, so that in my zeal I did not put an end to them. Therefore tell him I am making my covenant of peace with him. He and his descendants will have a covenant of a lasting priesthood, **because he was zealous for the honor of his God** and made atonement for the Israelites" (Numbers 25:5-13).

In this age we are to put away our swords (John 18:10-11) but not our zeal! Like Phinehas, we are to be zealous for the honor of God. We are called "ambassadors of Christ." We represent His Kingdom and bear His Name. We carry His treasure, the gospel of Jesus Christ. This treasure has infinite value because it cost Jesus His life. Because the blood of Jesus has infinite value, we must learn to regard His gospel as infinitely valuable to God. His honor is wrapped up in it. If we are angry because the person has *attacked us personally* or is mocking us just because we are "religious," that is no cause to withhold the gospel and shake the dust off our feet. But if a person begins to *mock God* and despise the message of Christ, we must not continue to explain the gospel to them lest it be trampled under their feet.

In order to discern when to shake the dust off our feet, we must walk humbly and be guided by the Holy Spirit. When we are ridiculed, it is very easy for us to react emotionally based upon fleshly desire for personal revenge. This is not what it means to be zealous for the honor of God. It is just a display of carnality that brings shame to the King we represent. So, we must be slow to the wrath that is produced by our own flesh, "...for man's anger does not bring about the righteous life that God desires" (James 1:20).

A righteous zeal for the honor of our God cannot be produced from our own power. It requires the supernatural power of the Holy Spirit. So, we must be under the control of the Spirit and in tune with His heart in order to know if and when to shake the dust from our feet. The more glorious the gospel is in our heart at the moment, the more likely we will be governed by the Holy Spirit in our preaching and discussions, for it is the Holy Spirit who makes the gospel glorious in our eyes. May God give us grace to comprehend the worth He places on the gospel so that we recognize our responsibility to withhold it on occasions when it (not us) is being ridiculed.

We should be cautious about addressing objections that people make to our message. If the person is sincerely considering Christ (by God's grace), then we should address issues that they are trying to sort through. For example, if a person has been under the false impression that the Bible is full of errors and not trustworthy, we can teach the facts about its historical accuracy or the integrity and age of the manuscripts. But if they are using objections as a means to defend their position of pride and unbelief, then we must humbly withdraw from the conversation.

Since we cannot see into the heart of the unbeliever, making a decision to withdraw from the conversation may be difficult. As best we can, we should attempt to discern whether they seem to be listening even if it seems they are responding negatively. If we elect to withdraw, we must not do so in retreat. We do so knowing in our hearts that at least for this moment, this person is not worthy to hear more about God's gracious Gift.

If we naively continue to counter their mental arguments, we run the risk of becoming partakers in a conversation that mocks Jesus. Since He is being ridiculed by this person's continued rejection, why should we even let the conversation continue? In the meantime, we can look for someone who is willing to hear the gospel and proclaim the glorious gospel to him since he will not mock it.

Don't wait to evangelize!

If you read every good book ever written on this subject, including the most important one, the Bible, you will not be able to learn how to evangelize without actually doing the work of evangelism. Without the experience of it, you will merely be a person full of head knowledge and you will never improve. The knowledge God gives must be put to use or it will be squandered. Jesus spoke many parables to warn us about the dangers of failing to fulfill our responsibility to steward the treasure He has entrusted to us. So read the Bible, read good books, but by all means do the work of evangelism lest you hear Him say on that day, *"You wicked, lazy servant! Take the talent from him and give it to the one who has the ten talents" (Matthew 25:26, 28)*. Remember that He also said, *"Everyone who has will be given more, and he will have an abundance. Whoever does not have, even what he has will be taken from him. And throw that worthless servant outside, into the darkness, where there will be weeping and gnashing of teeth" (Matthew 25:29-30)*.

Nobody begins evangelizing as an "expert." What qualifies a person to start? Has Jesus given you life from above and do you have a desire to spread the gospel? I encourage you to simply start doing it. Don't wait until you are an expert or you will never do it! Like the woman at the well (John 4), God can use you. (All she did was say, "Come and see a man who told me all that I ever did. Is this not the Messiah?") Even if you feel tongue-tied when you speak, God can still use you. In the biblical record, the disciples were uneducated but that did not stop them from opening their mouths about Christ. God can make us effective mouthpieces. *"Who gave man his mouth? Who makes him deaf or mute? Who gives him sight or makes him blind? Is it not I, the LORD? Now go; I will help you speak and will teach you what to say" (Exodus 4:11-12)*.

To prepare, take some time to examine the verses in the first two or three lessons of the "God's Redemption Message" study guide that you can download for free from the **Stones Cry Out web site.**[9] Write some of the references in the front of your Bible or better yet, commit some to memory. I recommend that you take it for a test drive by taking a child or young teen through it. Also, in **Appendix D**, another tool is provided to guide you through an informal, open **Bible gospel presentation using the book of Romans**. Remember that you can leave the person with a good tract that God can use to clarify the message further.

No matter how much you try to prepare yourself for the task of proclaiming the gospel, you eventually have to jump into the water and start swimming. Learning methods and memorizing scripture cannot fully prepare you for the task. As you gain more experience sharing the gospel, some of the things you memorized will become tools that the Holy Spirit will prompt you to use at just the right times. Until then, you need to keep sharing the gospel no matter how unnatural it might seem at times.

As you gain experience, remember to make a life-long commitment of following Jesus' example of proclaiming the gospel in situations that involve two-way dialog. If a man only speaks the gospel to crowds with no two-way dialog, he will be handicapped as an evangelist. A man can develop persuasive speaking skills that capture the attention of crowds, but not ever learn essential truth critical to communicating the gospel. Two-way gospel dialog is essential training for any man who wishes to do the work of an evangelist after the manner of Jesus and Paul. Without it, a man will never fully understand the importance of reasoning with people about sin, righteousness and judgment. A man may be convinced about these doctrines in his mind but until he learns how to reason with people face-to-face about them, he will not fully see them as indispensable for arousing a soul out of its slumber. All Christians that are serious about evangelism, including pastors, should make a habit of entering two-way gospel conversations and view them as essential ongoing training necessary to fulfill Jesus' call upon their lives.

---

[9] The Stones Cry Out web site is found at **www.StonesCryOut.INFO**. Go to the Free Evangelism Tools page selected from the top of the home page.

Do you feel completely inadequate for this task? That is good! It is best that we always feel inadequate for this task. This way, we are more likely to lean upon God to speak through us rather than rely on our own ability to speak. God gives us weakness in order to demonstrate His power and produce humility in us. We must view our inadequacy as a blessing and believe what God has said. We should adopt Paul's attitude: *"'My grace is sufficient for you, for my power is made perfect in weakness.' Therefore I will boast all the more gladly about my weaknesses, so that Christ's power may rest on me" (II Corinthians 12:9).* According to Paul, everything that is not done in faith is sin (Romans 14:23). This includes the preaching of the gospel. We must preach the gospel in faith believing that God wants it to go forth and that He is able to do it using us!

Suggestion: Try writing your own tracts as a means to learn how to better communicate the gospel.

Remember that Gospel proclamation is foundational.

There are many well-intentioned evangelical Christians and missionaries that believe it is appropriate and perhaps necessary to first develop friendships with people, hoping that eventually they will be able to share the gospel with them within the context of an established relationship. Some people go so far as to say that before we share the gospel with a person, we must first earn the right to do so by establishing a relationship with them. But what is the biblical pattern for establishing relationships with unbelievers that we intend to reach for Christ? If we do tell people up front that we are Christians, should we intentionally hold off discussing the gospel with them until the relationship is firmly established? Or should we be forthright about our faith in Christ and begin discussing the gospel from the very beginning of the relationship?

While God may not lead us to proclaim the gospel to each person we know or meet, the Bible teaches that we must be honest about our identity. And if the gospel is central in our lives, how could a truly meaningful relationship develop if we keep from talking about it? To do so, we would have to pretend that we are not enthralled with the person and work of Jesus. In the Bible record, whenever Jesus met someone, He was forthright about the things He believed and always sought to speak forth truth. Some have suggested that Jesus employed friendship evangelism with His disciples. I do not deny that Jesus formed intimate relationships with them, but He did so without hiding His intentions. With some of them, the first thing He said was, *"Follow me and I will make you fishers of men" (Matthew 4:19).*

The Apostle Paul normally sought out strangers for the purpose of reasoning with them from the scriptures about gospel truth. *"**As his custom was,** Paul went into the synagogue, and on three Sabbath days **He reasoned with them from the Scriptures**" (Acts 17:2).* He also went publicly from house to house (Acts 20:20). Often, he proclaimed his message in synagogues and was met with stiff opposition and persecution. His first order of business was to spread the gospel. He knew that some people would reject it and possibly mistreat him. But he knew that some would receive it. The relationships he built were based upon the knowledge of who he was and the message he preached. He did not first attempt to "win friends" in hope of sharing the gospel later. *"We speak as men approved by God to be entrusted with the gospel. **We are not trying to please men but God**" (I Thessalonians 2:4).*

There is no biblical record of Jesus or any of His apostles attempting to establish relationships with unbelievers while intentionally keeping their faith secret hoping to speak gospel truth to them later. Therefore, in our purposeful efforts to make disciples, let us be forthright about our identity as Christians and pray for opportunities to share our testimony and gospel truth with the unbelievers we seek to befriend.

Be encouraged as you sow.

I know someone that attends an evangelical church in a town near us. On occasion, she tells us the number of people who were saved during their past Sunday morning service. Sometimes ten, and sometimes twenty or more people "get saved." Have you ever heard stories of dozens of people "getting saved" each week in a church in your town? Have you ever heard someone talk about a recent evangelism experience that involved several people "getting saved?"

I am not saying that there are not situations somewhere in the world in which many people get saved at one time. But we need to be aware of the fact that many Christians think they have successfully evangelized if they can get a person to say a "sinner's prayer." They work out clever schemes that walk a person through a series of thoughts framed in such a way that only a fool would decline the invitation to pray a prayer to "be saved." Most of the people that pray these prayers remain dead in their sins. Yet, they are given false assurance that their sins have been forgiven. Such practices are completely unbiblical and, in my opinion, dangerous. If you have read this far and embraced what this book teaches, then you will not engage in such practices. But you will also not see as many so-called "conversions."

It is highly unusual for people to begin believing the first time they mentally understand the gospel. Most people remain under conviction of sin for days, weeks, months or even years before they repent and believe. You must learn to be like a farmer who patiently waits for his crops to grow. I write this to give you encouragement in your waiting. While it is true that God is the only One who can produce new life, we can be assured that since it is God's desire to advance His Kingdom, He will undoubtedly bring it about. Let me tell two stories that illustrate this.

When my wife and I were brand new believers, we owned a house with a swimming pool. There were several neighborhood children who wanted to swim in our pool. We told them that if they were to swim in the pool, they would first have to memorize a new verse of scripture and recite it to us each day they wanted to swim. (We gave them specific verses from Romans and John.) Over twenty years later, we ran into one of them, now all grown. She was excited to see us and exclaimed that she and her sister were now believers and actively involved in a Bible-believing church. Then she said, "It was those verses!" Every time I think of this, my heart is warmed. This story reminds me that God is the One who gives the increase and the gospel is powerful to save.

I can relate another story that demonstrates the same thing. About three years ago, I met a Muslim man living in Dearborn. It was difficult for us to communicate because his English was poor back then. But he managed to tell me that he used to own a Bible but he left it in Lebanon. I gave him a new Arabic Bible but I don't think he read much of it, if any. I continued to see him on occasion and tried to communicate gospel truth each time. But each attempt seemed ineffective due to the language barrier. About a year later, I learned that he had broken his hip and was in the hospital near my house. I went to visit him and gave him an Arabic gospel of John. Since he was so isolated in the hospital, he ended up reading it several times.

Several weeks later, I visited him again at his house. In the best way he could, he tried to tell me that Jesus is now his God. Due to the language barrier, it was difficult to know what had happened in his heart. But I offered him a complete Arabic New Testament. About 3 months later, I stopped by again to visit. I asked, "Do you ever read the New Testament I gave to you." He got up, hobbled over to the mantle, picked it up, kissed it and said, "About three to four hours." After asking for clarification, he indicated that he was reading it about three to four hours each day!

From both these stories, we see that God is able to save through His powerful gospel. We see also that He can do it without our "expert" help. We also see that it is difficult to know what is happening with the gospel seed in some people. Yet, since it is God who gives the increase, we can be assured that the seed will produce the harvest He desires. Sometimes it may take years but God's timing is best and brings Him the most glory. Though I try to faithfully water the seed and be there to watch it grow, in many cases, God has other plans that are better than mine. I have discussed the gospel at great length with many people that I may never see again in this life. Yet, in the end, I am confident that I will see some of their faces at that glorious wedding feast of the Lamb. Let us rejoice in the privilege of proclaiming the gospel and look forward to fully understanding God's purposes clearly on that day.

For more encouragement and inspiration to evangelize, read my book, *Evangelism Fuel, Motivation to Evangelize,* described in the *Other Books by Tom Bear* section near the back of this book.

Water the Gospel Seed.

Generally, evangelism requires multiple discussions during which gospel seeds are planted and watered. This is how Jesus worked. He spoke often in parables to convey one truth at a time. This truth would then be given opportunity to germinate. In the twenty-first century, some people might classify this as "discipleship" training. I simply call it watering the gospel seed.

To be a faithful steward and a person who cares, we should ask the hearer for the opportunity to talk with him again about the gospel. We should hope that our initial discussion was merely the beginning of a long-term friendship founded upon the full knowledge that we are followers of Jesus that want others to enjoy the treasure we have found in Him. If the person is hesitant to allow us this privilege, it may be a sign that he is really not interested. He may not be someone that we should spend much time with in the future. If he agrees, he still might not be all that interested but at least an invitation has been gained to contact him again.

If God is drawing a person to Christ, he may or may not be interested in attending a regular meeting of believers (like a church service). Yet, he may likely be open to having a one-on-one Bible study with you. If he is willing to have a one-on-one Bible study with you, I highly recommend that you use "God's Redemption Message" study guide that you can download for free from the **Stones Cry Out web site.**[10] If a person goes through this material and comprehends what the Bible says in the verses contained in it, he will have a strong mental understanding of the Gospel and many foundational truths about God.

---

[10] The Stones Cry Out web site is found at **www.StonesCryOut.INFO**. Go to the Free Evangelism Tools page selected from the top of the home page.

A person may acquire a strong intellectual understanding of the gospel but not yet "believe from the heart." Yet, he may be willing to join a group Bible study or home church. This would be excellent. But if he resists joining a group of believers and is still interested in learning more, you may want to consider a study of the Old Testament. I realize that many Christians would balk at this idea, but I can tell you with all authority that it is a good idea. The Apostle Paul said that the Old Testament Scriptures are able to make a person wise for salvation through faith in Christ Jesus (see II Timothy 3:15). You might consider reading and discussing a chapter of the Old Testament each time you meet, especially Genesis and some of the Messianic prophecies.

Note: If you are working with a Muslim that seems genuinely interested in learning the gospel, you might want to consider giving him a copy of my book, *The Way to Heaven, The Difference Between Islam and Christianity* described in the *Other Books by Tom Bear* section near the back of this book.

Harvest the crop.

Jesus often used figurative language to teach spiritual truth. The following words of His underscore the goal of our evangelizing.

By their fruit you will recognize them. Do people pick grapes from thornbushes, or figs from thistles? Likewise every good tree bears good fruit, but a bad tree bears bad fruit. A good tree cannot bear bad fruit, and a bad tree cannot bear good fruit. Every tree that does not bear good fruit is cut down and thrown into the fire. Thus, by their fruit you will recognize them. "Not everyone who says to me, `Lord, Lord,' will enter the Kingdom of heaven, but only he who does the will of my Father who is in heaven. Many will say to me on that day, `Lord, Lord, did we not prophesy in your name, and in your name drive out demons and perform many miracles?' Then I will tell them plainly, `I never knew you. Away from me, you evildoers!' (Matthew 7:16-23).

The outcome we desire is true fruit of the Kingdom: radically changed lives. We want to see people rescued from the kingdom of darkness and transferred into the Kingdom of Jesus. We want to see God change dead people into those who worship Him in spirit and in truth.

Since we are merely people, we cannot look into the hearts of those who hear our message to know if they are truly trusting in the sacrificial work of Jesus. We cannot know for sure if they have come to know Him. To properly care for them, we must patiently continue watering the seed and encourage them to believe God's message of redemption through Jesus. As we observe what appears to be God's work in them, it is important to remember that salvation is by grace through faith and not a result of walking an aisle or praying a prayer.

Know what people must do to be saved.

There are millions of people who falsely think they are Christians simply because they repeated a "sinner's prayer" or walked down to the front of an auditorium at the invitation of an evangelist. They remain dead in their trespasses and sins. Yet, they falsely believe they are Christians. They followed the promise of a man rather than believing the promise of God. The man told them they would be saved if they repeated a "sinner's prayer" or walked down an aisle. God makes no such promise. His promise is *"Believe on the Lord Jesus Christ and you will be saved" (Acts 16:31)*. While most people do not know what it means to believe on the Lord Jesus Christ, we should not veer from God's prescription. We should teach them what it means to believe rather than confuse the issue with unbiblical promises.

Natural man refuses to believe that he is helpless and unable to do something to merit salvation (Ephesians 2:1-9). This is why the preaching of the cross is foolishness to him (I Corinthians 1:18). If we tell him he can be saved by repeating a "sinner's prayer," he naturally grabs on to it as something he can **do**. It is a ritual that he understands and for most, it involves no cost.

As we present the gospel, it is critical that we avoid the possibility of leading someone astray. We must make clear that people are justified by faith alone. We must NEVER instruct a person to repeat a canned prayer as the means "to receive Christ." I strongly recommend that you avoid telling sinners to do anything that is not specified in the Bible.

So, what does the Bible say that we can tell sinners? I suggest that Romans 12:1 sheds some light. *"I beseech you therefore, brethren, by the mercies of God, that you present your bodies a living sacrifice, holy, acceptable to God, which is your reasonable service."* Paul said that in response to God's offer of salvation, a person should offer himself without reservation to God. This is a demonstration that the person really believes what God has said. ALL who truly believe the gospel will automatically surrender their lives to Jesus. If a person is unwilling to surrender his life to Jesus, it proves he does not yet believe the gospel. Surrendering itself does not justify the person. He is justified the moment he first believes. (He is justified by faith alone.) But because he truly believes from the heart, he gladly surrenders his life to Jesus. His believing is the cause. His surrendering is the effect of believing.

You should not lead a person in prayer to force this. He must voluntarily offer his life to God. He does not need special instructions about which words to use. That is not important at all. The question at hand is who will be his Lord from now on? Is he willing to let Jesus be his Lord from now on? Is he willing to take Jesus' yoke upon him or not? If he really believes the gospel, he will gladly surrender his life to Jesus. He will gladly follow Him instead of running his own life. The type of surrender that Jesus wants is one that involves the heart. Words in a canned prayer mean nothing. This type of surrender is something he must begin doing and continue doing until he dies.

To help a person understand the idea of total surrender, I suggest we preach that genuine faith always embraces the true cost of being Jesus' disciple, the loss of our lives unto Him. I also suggest that we tell them that, as those who have surrendered their lives to Jesus, they should show their allegiance to Him by being baptized. If you still believe that a person must say a sinner's prayer in order to "receive Christ," I urge you to read **Appendix B, *"What does it mean to call upon the Lord?"***

Discern when a sinner starts believing in Christ.

In reality, we simply do not know for sure if and when a person has started believing the gospel "from the heart." Yet, there are some characteristics that will surface in the life of a person who truly believes.

Let us consider how the Bible defines "repentance" and how it relates to the term "believe." *"After John the Baptist had been taken into custody, Jesus was* **preaching the gospel** *of God saying,* **'The time is fulfilled, and the Kingdom of God is at hand; repent and believe the gospel'"** *(Mark 1:14-15).* Is it possible for a person to obey Jesus' command to "repent" and yet not "believe the gospel?" What does it mean to repent? Some believe that to repent means to experience feelings of regret, remorse or sorrow. There are also many who believe it means to get rid of sin or "clean up" one's life. This study will first demonstrate that these views are not what Jesus had in mind when He told the people to repent. Then, a biblical portrayal of repentance will be presented.

Repentance is not to be equated with mere feelings of remorse or regret or sorrow.

Many words in the English language have multiple meanings and often convey only vague ideas. But the Greek words chosen by the New Testament writers relating to this subject convey precise ideas. Therefore, to show that repentance leading to salvation is not mere feelings of remorse, regret or sorrow, we will consider a few of the Greek words used by the New Testament authors relating to this subject. Rather than provide an exhaustive survey of the New Testament's use of these words, this study will primarily focus on one passage: II Corinthians 7:8-10. An examination of more passages will only serve to underscore what is evident from the II Corinthians 7 passage. The following Greek words will be considered:

metanoeo: translated "repent" in the NASB[5], used 34 times in the Greek New Testament. This is the word used in the gospels to record Jesus' command to "repent and believe the gospel." It is the word that depicts the repentance leading to salvation.

metanoia: the noun form of the verb **metanoeo** (above), translated "repentance" in the NASB, used 24 times in the Greek New Testament.

metamellomai: translated "repent" in the KJV but "<u>regret</u>" or "remorse" in the NASB, used 5 times in the Greek New Testament

lupee: usually translated "<u>sorrow</u>," used 15 times in the Greek New Testament.

> For though I caused you sorrow by my letter, I do not regret (metamellomai) it; though I did regret (metamellomai) it—for I see that that letter caused you sorrow, though only for a while— I now rejoice, not that you were made sorrowful, but that you were made sorrowful to the point of repentance (metanoia); for you were made sorrowful according to the will of God, so that you might not suffer loss in anything through us. For the sorrow (lupee) that is according to the will of God produces a repentance (metanoia) without regret, leading to salvation, but the sorrow (lupee) of the world produces death (II Corinthians 7:8-10).

In this passage, Paul uses the Greek word _metamellomai_ twice in verse eight to describe his feelings of regret over the writing of his letter. In verses nine and ten, he uses the Greek word metanoia which the NASB translates as "repentance" (leading to salvation). These two Greek words have similar roots but _metanoia_ ("repentance" NASB) conveys a different concept than _metamellomai_ ("regret" NASB).   Paul also uses the word _lupee_ to describe the emotion of sorrow. **The fact that Paul uses each of these words to convey concepts that are distinct from each other indicates that repentance leading to salvation is not mere feelings of regret, remorse or sorrow.**

It can be further noted that every time the Greek word _metamellomai_ is used throughout the New Testament, it conveys a feeling of remorse or regret and it is <u>never</u> used to depict the type of repentance leading to salvation. For example, this word is used to convey the feelings Judas had after he betrayed Jesus. _"Then when Judas, who betrayed Him, saw that He_ (Jesus) _had been condemned, he_ (Judas) _felt remorse and returned the thirty pieces of silver to the chief priests and elders" (Matthew 27:3 NASB)._ We know from Jesus' testimony in Matthew 26:4 that Judas was condemned. This proves it is possible to experience sincere feelings of remorse but fail to repent.

It can also be noted that every time the Greek word *lupee* (noun) or its verb form *lupeo* is used, they are <u>never</u> used to convey "repentance" leading to salvation. They are always used to convey the emotion of grief or sorrow. In the II Corinthians 7:8-10 passage, only sorrow that is *"according to the will of God"* produces repentance leading to salvation, while sorrow *"of the world"* produces death. So, sorrow in and of itself is not repentance. Lastly, it should be noted that the Greek word *metanoia* and its verb form *metanoeo* are both used exclusively by the New Testament writers to convey repentance leading to salvation. From this brief survey, we may conclude that repentance leading to salvation is not mere feelings of regret, remorse or sorrow.

Repentance is not just "cleaning up" one's life.

This portion of our survey will demonstrate that repentance is also something different than self-reformation. The New Testament makes clear that repentance produces fruit in the form of good works.

*So, King Agrippa, I did not prove disobedient to the heavenly vision, but kept declaring both to those of Damascus first, and also at Jerusalem and then throughout all the region of Judea, and even to the Gentiles, that they should repent and turn to God, performing **deeds appropriate to repentance** (Acts 26:19-20).*

While it cannot be denied that when repentance occurs, good deeds become evident in the life of the one who repents, it is critical to define what is meant by good deeds. The Bible indicates that unregenerate man cannot perform what God considers good deeds. Paul said, *"...everything that does not come from faith is sin" (Romans 14:23).* The unregenerate man does not possess faith. He remains dead in his trespasses and sins because God has not given him faith (Ephesians 2:1-9). An unregenerate man could work hard to produce food for his family. The world would consider this noble and would never classify such activity as sin. But God does because the one working is considered by God to be wicked and the work he is doing falls short of the glory of God. It does not honor God. He works to make way for the continuance of his life. The fact that his family might benefit from it also serves his purpose because the suffering or death of his family would cause him great sorrow. He is living a life that revolves around himself rather than living solely for God and doing all to His glory. This dishonors God. It is all done to satisfy man's interest, without regard to God's desire. This is why Isaiah could say, ***"All our righteous deeds are like a filthy garment" (Isaiah 64:6).*** This is exactly how God views the works of man when they are produced independent of God's enabling power. Only works that have their source of power in God actually bring glory to Him and qualify as "good deeds." This is why Jesus could say, *"But whoever lives by the truth comes into the light, so that it may be seen plainly that what he has done has been done through God" (John 3:21).*

In contrast to those who come "into the light," John the Baptist met up with those who, being a brood of vipers, as he called them, had not come into the light. To these religious leaders he said, *"You brood of vipers! Who warned you to flee from the coming wrath? Produce fruit in keeping with repentance. And do not think you can say to yourselves, `We have Abraham as our father.' I tell you that out of these stones God can raise up children for Abraham. The ax is already at the root of the trees, and every tree that does not produce good fruit will be cut down and thrown into the fire" (Matthew 3:7-10).* John told the Pharisees that if they were going to escape the coming wrath, fruit that is associated with repentance would have to be displayed in their life. He warned them (and us) that if no such fruit were produced in their lives, they would be thrown into the fire.

The type of fruit John the Baptist had in mind is the good deeds that the Apostle John described *as having been wrought in God (John 3:31NASB)* This is in keeping with Jesus' teaching using the analogy of the vine and branches. *"I am the vine; you are the branches. If a man remains in me and I in him, he will bear much fruit; **apart from me you can do nothing**. If anyone does not remain in me, he is like a branch that is thrown away and withers; such branches are picked up, thrown into the fire and burned. If you remain in me and my words remain in you, ask whatever you wish, and it will be given you. This is to my Father's glory, **that you bear much fruit, showing yourselves to be my disciples"** (John 15:5-8).* Jesus did not mean that apart from Him, people could not go to work and earn a living. What He was saying is that apart from Him, they could do nothing that actually pleases God and brings Him glory. Nothing that is done in our strength honors God in the least. This is why Jesus said, *"The Spirit gives life; the flesh counts for nothing" (John 6:63).* So, John the Baptist was warning the Pharisees that their entire way of viewing God and themselves was completely opposite of the way God viewed them. They saw themselves as having righteousness on their own merit while John the Baptist saw them as a brood of vipers.

This contrast is vividly seen in the parable Jesus told about the sinner and the publican:

Two men went up to the temple to pray, one a Pharisee and the other a tax collector. The Pharisee stood up and prayed about himself: `God, I thank you that I am not like other men--robbers, evildoers, adulterers-- or even like this tax collector. I fast twice a week and give a tenth of all I get.' But the tax collector stood at a distance. He would not even look up to heaven, but beat his breast and said, `God, have mercy on me, a sinner.' I tell you that this man, rather than the other, went home justified before God. For everyone who exalts himself will be humbled, and he who humbles himself will be exalted (Luke 18:9-14).

Though this passage does not actually employ the word repentance, it is clear that the publican experienced it. Unlike the Pharisee, he suddenly saw himself as a sinner alienated from the holy God by a wicked, self-driven, self-seeking life. While he had feelings of remorse over his sin, it is the change in his view about himself and God that actually gave room for his remorse. The Pharisee on the other hand, remained entrenched in his dependence on his own goodness. He did not see himself the way God saw him and he did not understand God the way He really is, perfect in holiness and intolerant of sin. It is this notion that a man can somehow clean up his life to become acceptable to God that is actually a most putrid manifestation of wickedness and it is extremely offensive to God. This attitude is one of pride that belittles the righteousness of God. When a man falsely thinks his own righteousness makes him acceptable to God, that man is elevated in his own eyes and God is made out to be less than perfectly righteous. God's righteousness is <u>PERFECT</u>. He cannot judge according to human standards. He cannot accept plea bargains. When a man thinks his own righteousness makes him acceptable to God, he presumes that God can bend His standard of perfect righteousness/justice for him and not mete out the punishment demanded by that perfect righteousness. If God were to do this, He would cease being perfectly righteous. *"For the LORD your God is God of gods and Lord of lords, the great God, mighty and awesome, who shows no partiality and accepts no bribes" (Deut. 10:17). The LORD is upright; He is my Rock, and there is **no** unrighteousness in him" (Psalm 92:15). "Your eyes are too pure to look on evil; you cannot tolerate wrong" (Habakkuk 1:13).*

Jesus identified this problem in which people mistakenly view themselves as righteous as one that is deep within the human heart. *"Woe to you, teachers of the law and Pharisees, you hypocrites! You clean the outside of the cup and dish, but inside they are full of greed and self-indulgence. Blind Pharisee! First clean the inside of the cup and dish, and then the outside also will be clean" (Matthew 23:25).* Jesus' teaching helps us understand the nature of repentance leading to salvation. The Pharisees thought they attained righteousness by keeping the law. They were blind to the fact that they were failing to keep it. They mistakenly reduced the demands of the law to that which was outwardly doable and believed they were acceptable to God because of their religious status and relative goodness in comparison to those less religious. But according to Jesus' diagnosis, unrighteousness was gushing forth from their hearts making them unrighteous in God's sight.

If a person thinks he can actually "clean up" his life to get right with God, he has not experienced repentance. It is this very attitude that changes when we repent. Repentance causes us to view things differently so that we stop seeing ourselves as righteous enough or able to make ourselves righteous enough to merit acceptance in the sight of the righteous God. Jesus said, *"I say to you that unless your righteousness surpasses that of the scribes and Pharisees, you will not enter the Kingdom of heaven" (Matthew 5:20).* The inside of the cup must first be cleansed. That is, God Himself must supernaturally regenerate the heart first. Then true righteousness (fruit) will be produced in our lives and we can follow Jesus' instruction, *"Let your light shine before men in such a way that they may see your good works, and glorify your Father who is in heaven" (Matt 5:13-16).* While Jesus condemned the wicked notion that a man can live righteously in his own power, He taught that by God's power, His disciples will indeed live righteously, not out of a sense of duty but from new hearts of love for their heavenly Father.

In their own power, nobody can live righteous lives as Jesus defined righteousness. But as Jesus once said, *"With man this is impossible, but with God all things are possible" (Matthew 19:26).* It is God's intention to conform Jesus' disciples into the very image of Jesus so that the world will see the light of Jesus shining through them (true righteousness) even in this life. If a man claims to be His disciple while at the same time living a life that is not characterized by this righteousness, he should question whether he is truly His disciple. *"Beware of the false prophets, who come to you in sheep's clothing, but inwardly are ravenous wolves. You will know them by their fruits. Grapes are not gathered from thorn bushes nor figs from thistles, are they? So every good tree bears good fruit, but the bad tree bears bad fruit. A good tree cannot produce bad fruit, nor can a bad tree produce good fruit. Every tree that does not bear good fruit is cut down and thrown into the fire. So then, you will know them by their fruits" (Matthew 6:15-20).* Jesus went on to warn His listeners, *"Not everyone who says to Me, 'Lord, Lord,' will enter the Kingdom of heaven, but he who does the will of My Father who is in heaven will enter. Many will say to Me on that day, 'Lord, Lord, did we not prophesy in Your name, and in Your name cast out demons, and in Your name perform many miracles?' And then I will declare to them, 'I never knew you; DEPART FROM ME, YOU WHO PRACTICE LAWLESSNESS' " (Matthew 6:21-23).*

While this may seem like digression, it all pertains to the subject of repentance. Jesus taught that His disciples' lives would be characterized by a righteousness that unmistakably could not be produced by man, but by God alone (Romans 8:4, John 14:21, 23; 15:5). For this to happen in the life of a person, repentance is absolutely necessary. A person must abandon the notion that he can stand before God in his own righteousness and believe rather that he can do nothing to help himself. As we will see, this change in perspective is not something that takes place by the will of man.

Biblical portrayal of repentance (metanoia)

Before beginning this portion of the study, let me set forth the following definition of repentance:

Repentance (*metanoia*): The supernatural change in a man's heart and mind that accompanies regeneration and results in a desire to live for God's pleasure and purposes rather than his own because he believes what God has revealed to him about Himself.

The following biblical analysis and discussion is presented to demonstrate that:

- Repentance is the appropriate response to the gospel message.
- When a sinner repents, justification/reconciliation occurs.
- Where there is no repentance, there will be no salvation.
- Repentance is nothing less than the supernatural work of God.

Repentance is the appropriate response to the gospel.

When asked, "What must we do to be saved?," the apostles often replied, "Believe on the Lord Jesus Christ and you will be saved" (Acts 16:31). John put it this way, *"This is His commandment, that we believe in the name of His Son, Jesus Christ" (I John 3:23).* We conclude that God has invited and commanded people to believe in the name of His Son, Jesus Christ. Yet, often the apostles replied with words like, *"Repent and return, so that your sins may be wiped away" (Acts 3:19).* And just as we are commanded to believe, Paul states that all are commanded to repent, *"God is now declaring to men that all people everywhere should repent" (Acts 17:30).*

Though the word for believe is different than the word for repent, both are said to result in the remission of sins and both seem to be appropriate responses to the gospel. Jesus used both words together to instruct His hearers, *"The time is fulfilled, and the Kingdom of God is at hand; repent and believe in the gospel" (Mark 1:15).* The command to repent in response to the gospel is recorded in numerous passages (Matthew 4:17, Mark 1:15; 6:12; Acts 2:38; 3:19). Though repentance is something different than believing, these passages suggest that they are tied tightly together. Both result in remission of sins and both are linked to salvation. We know that nobody can be saved without believing on Jesus, the only Savior given by God for the salvation of sinners. We will see later that likewise, nobody can be saved who does not repent. Both are essential to our salvation.

When a sinner repents, justification/reconciliation occurs.

In Luke 15:7, Jesus said that there is great rejoicing in heaven when a sinner repents. From this statement, we claim that whenever a sinner repents, he is justified and reconciled to God. In contrast, there is no rejoicing in heaven if someone merely has feelings of remorse over his sins. There is no rejoicing in heaven if someone attempts to "clean up" his life. No! The rejoicing takes place when a sinner is delivered out of the kingdom of darkness! Nothing less will do. God does not save in steps or by twisting of arms and manipulation. When God saves, it is always miraculous and complete and it is a sinner's complete deliverance that causes the glory of God to shine and heaven to rejoice, nothing less. Thus we conclude that when sinners repent, justification and reconciliation occurs.

Where there is no repentance, there will be no salvation.

> *"I tell you, no, but unless you repent, you will all likewise perish" (Luke 13:3).*

If a person does not repent, then he retains the mindset that he had from the beginning. God calls this mindset wicked. It exalts itself above the need for salvation and belittles the righteousness of God. This mindset always seeks its own happiness and way of life independent from God and without regard for what He thinks and desires. It does not see the glory in Christ as the Wonderful Savior because it does not really see the need for a savior as God declares the need. As long as a person has this mindset, he cannot be saved because Jesus came to save sinners, not the "righteous" (those who mistakenly see themselves as righteous enough to stand before God). Therefore, as Jesus said, *"...unless they repent, they will perish."*

Repentance is nothing less than the supernatural work of God.

As we see from Acts 17:30, "God commands men everywhere to repent." Likewise, God has issued a command for all men to believe the gospel. God holds men accountable for their response to these commands. If they do not heed the commands, they justly remain under condemnation. As is the case with all of God's commands, the natural man simply refuses to obey them because they run contrary to his sinful desires. So, just as man will not believe, he likewise will not repent, simply because he does not want to do so. Ephesians 2:8 says, "It is by grace you have been saved, through faith--and this not from yourselves, it is the gift of God." Faith is seen here as a gift that God gives to a sinner so that he believes and is saved.

It is God that gives a person the power to believe. Likewise, repentance is something that God grants or gives. In the parable of the rich man and Lazarus in Luke 16, the rich man wants Abraham to send Lazarus to his brothers to warn them about hell.

"And he said, 'Then I beg you, father, that you send him to my father's house—for I have five brothers—in order that he may warn them, so that they will not also come to this place of torment.' But Abraham said, 'They have Moses and the Prophets; let them hear them.' "But he said, 'No, father Abraham, but if someone goes to them from the dead, they will repent!' But he said to him, 'If they do not listen to Moses and the Prophets, they will not be persuaded even if someone rises from the dead'" (Luke 16:27-31).

Notice Abraham's response. He said that even if someone goes to them from the dead, they would not heed the warning. A person's sinful heart is darkened and being wicked, it wants no part of God, even if the person happens to be "religious" in the same way the Pharisees were religious. This holds true for many people today that attend church religiously but have no life of God in them.

Paul states that the *"...the kindness of God leads you to repentance" (Romans 2:4).* This gives strong indication that God, out of His kindness, does something to bring people to repentance. We see this theme repeated in the disciple's response to the story of the conversion of Gentiles while Peter preached. *"When they (the disciples) heard this* (testimony from Peter), *they quieted down and glorified God, saying, 'Well then, God has <u>granted</u> to the Gentiles also the repentance that leads to life'" (Acts 11:18).* The disciples understood repentance as something that God "grants" or gives. Paul also considered repentance something that God gives. *"The Lord's bond-servant must not be quarrelsome, but be kind to all, able to teach, patient when wronged, with gentleness correcting those who are in opposition, if perhaps God may <u>grant</u> them repentance leading to the knowledge of the truth, and they may come to their senses and escape from the snare of the devil, having been held captive by him to do his will" (II Timothy 2:24-26).*

According to Ephesians 2:1, people who have not come to Christ are dead in their trespasses and sins. Paul says in I Corinthians 1:18 that, *"The word of the cross is foolishness to those who are perishing, but to us who are being saved it is the power of God."* He also said, *"The natural man does not accept the things of the Spirit of God, for they are foolishness to him; and he cannot understand them, because they are spiritually appraised" (I Corinthians 2:14).* Because of man's wicked, independent heart, he simply will not repent. He will continue to rely on his own way of looking at things. He will continue to consider himself sufficiently righteous to gain acceptance by God and believe that God would be unjust to condemn him on judgment day. He refuses to consider the holiness of God, the depth of his sin and his absolute need of a Savior. <u>The only way he will repent and believe is if God gives him this power</u> because it is not something he will do on his own.

In summary, repentance leading to salvation is not mere feelings of regret, remorse or sorrow. Repentance is not just "cleaning up one's life" or an attempt of self-reformation. As we have observed here, repentance leading to salvation is a supernatural change of mind and heart that causes a man to abandon forever all hope of God's approval on the basis of his own righteousness or good deeds, so that he begins to rely fully on the finished work of Christ in his behalf.

Repentance causes a man to agree with God's declaration about Himself:
- He is perfectly righteous and rightly offended at his sins.
- He is just to condemn him to eternal punishment for his sins against Him.

Repentance produces agreement with God's declaration about his condemnation:
- His sin makes him guilty before the righteous God.
- The just sentence for his sins is eternal punishment away from God's presence.

Repentance produces a genuine humility that causes a person to see God and himself rightly, thus showing the need for God to save him from his helpless predicament. Repentance recognizes Jesus as the perfect and only remedy for his condemned condition since He is God's appointed Savior. The natural man will never repent, but when God regenerates a person, he is given supernatural power to believe. Because he believes, he turns from his former manner of living (repents) and begins living for God's pleasure and purposes.

Baptize them and teach them to observe all things.

When a man comes to faith in Christ, Jesus said we are to baptize them and teach them to observe all things (Matthew 28:19). A man's unwillingness to be baptized may be evidence that true repentance has not taken place. Baptism is a picture that portrays how God saves people. God causes sinners to become fully identified with Christ's death, burial and resurrection. When a man trusts in Christ, he loses the life that he held so dear and is supernaturally raised to new life with a heart of loving obedience to God. Water baptism is a way for the new believer to show his old friends and new brothers and sisters in Christ and the host of heaven, that by God's grace, he died to his old life and now lives to God.

From the historical record of Acts and the information provided in the epistles, we know that all disciples of Christ are "added to the Church." (See Acts 2:42.) This book focuses on the making of disciples and therefore does not address the principles of church life. But we must always remember that God's purpose in making disciples is to build His Church with the goal that She will one day be presented to the Lamb as His Bride. Therefore, the job of making disciples is not completed until a man is converted, baptized and "added to the Church." The Bible teaches that all true disciples are added to the universal, invisible Church of Christ the moment they are baptized into Christ by the Holy Spirit (I Corinthians 12:13). If a man has been raised from spiritual death to life in Christ, he is in Christ, a part of His Body.

Therefore, it is a contradiction if a man claims to be in Christ and yet is not attached to the physical body of Christ through a local church. Certainly, we will wonder about the reality of his faith if he does not manifest a love for the brethren. *"If anyone says, "I love God," yet hates his brother, he is a liar. For anyone who does not love his brother, whom he has seen, cannot love God, whom he has not seen"* (I John 4:20). Therefore, we desire that the hearts of new believers become knit to other Christians and that they learn to serve alongside them in the work of the Kingdom.

If the new believer is from our culture, it probably makes sense to invite him to our own local church if it is near enough to where he lives. But if the person is from a different culture, it would probably be better for him to become knit to believers of his own culture, especially if he struggles with the English language. Our primary concern is that the new believer finds nourishment for his soul and becomes united with other believers in following Christ. We must diligently seek God's mind and be open to God's direction concerning the integration of each new believer into a group of believers that follow Christ. Some considerations concerning this are discussed in **Appendix C,** *"Integrating New Believers into Local Churches."*

Section 3: Expect Opposition!

Expect satanic opposition.
Resign yourself to a life of rejection.
Know the reason the world hates us.
Be prepared for cultural clashes.

Expect satanic opposition

Let me preface this section with a word of warning to all who take seriously our Lord's commission to advance His Kingdom through the proclamation of His gospel:

Be On the Alert!

"Your enemy the devil prowls around like a roaring lion looking for someone to devour" (I Peter 5:8).

God has graciously reminded me of the dangers at hand and impressed upon me that it is time to increase our awareness of the warfare directed against God's Kingdom so that we might realize our great need for God's protection and deliverance in the battle set before us.

As we know, YHWH, the true and living God, is jealous of His Name. We are his feeble servants. By commissioning us mere people to go forth to proclaim His Name as His ambassadors, He has put His Name on the line. I ask you now, if you were Satan, what would your chief objectives and strategies be? Where would you concentrate your forces? Have you thought about this?

You may not sense it at times, but great wickedness is plotted against those in God's Kingdom. Paul knew this very well. The intensity of his experience as one who advanced God's Kingdom gave him insight into the spiritual warfare being waged by the forces of Satan. This knowledge enabled him to say, *"We are not unaware of his schemes" (II Corinthians 2:11).* Like Paul, we should not be ignorant of his schemes. I ask you again, what would your plan of attack be and where would you direct your forces to attack? Let us consider the nature of the enemy. What is it that motivates him to fight in the first place? What are his overall objectives? Let us consider the chief enemy. He is the vile father of lies and hater of God.

It is his vile hate for God that motivates him. His hatred was present at the cross and it was he that moved the onlookers to express his hatred for the Christ:

*"The people stood watching, and the rulers even **sneered at him**. They said, 'He saved others; let him save himself if he is the Christ of God, the Chosen One.' The soldiers also came up and **mocked him**. They offered him wine vinegar and said, 'If you are the king of the Jews, save yourself'"* (Luke 23:35&36).

He is the spirit that now works in the children of disobedience to rebel against the Most High God:

*"The kings of the earth **take their stand** and the rulers **gather together against the LORD and against his Anointed One**. "Let us break their chains," they say, "and **throw off their fetters**." The One enthroned in heaven laughs; the Lord scoffs at them. Then he rebukes them in his anger and terrifies them in his wrath"* (Psalm 2:2 –5).

His delight to get people to curse God is evidenced by his strong desire and attempt to cause Job to curse God. Satan said to God,

"He will surely curse you to your face" (Job 2:4).

His great wickedness is observed in his desire to be God.

*"**I will ascend** to heaven; **I will raise my throne above the stars of God**; **I will sit enthroned** on the mount of assembly, on the utmost heights of the sacred mountain. **I will ascend** above the tops of the clouds; **I will make myself like the Most High**"* (Isaiah 14:13-14).

Do these verses remind you of his extreme hatred for God? Can you hear him sneering vile abominations against Him? Do you see how he wants to malign the Name of God and blind people from seeing truth? *"The god of this age has blinded the minds of unbelievers, so that they cannot see the light of the gospel of the glory of Christ, who is the image of God" (II Corinthians 4:4).* In light of his wicked hatred for God and desire to malign His Name, where do you think he would direct his efforts in the theater of battle? Though he hates all Christians, he does not need to focus his attack on Christians and ministries that are not significantly proclaiming the gospel because it is **the gospel** that is the power of God unto salvation. While Satan is opposed to all of God's people and various ministries, gospel proclamation represents the greatest threat against his kingdom because the gospel is **THE** means God has chosen to advance His Kingdom.

The degree to which a Christian or ministry may play a role in the advancement of God's Kingdom is directly tied to the amount of gospel being proclaimed. I state, therefore, that Satan is focusing most of his forces against those Christians and ministries that are most actively proclaiming the gospel of our Lord Jesus Christ. In Satan's mind, Christians not actively proclaiming the gospel are already defeated and need none of his attention.

These wicked forces are not fighting without emotion. They hate us with the same vile hatred they have for God. They sneer at us. They are cursing us to our face. They take their stand against us and are gathered together to destroy us in order that the gospel remains veiled. In light of this, let me remind you that *"our struggle is not against flesh and blood, but against the rulers, against the powers, against the world forces of this darkness, against the spiritual forces of wickedness in the heavenly places" (Ephesians 6:12).*

Of all people, we should take this the most seriously. After all, we are of the unskilled and feeble sort. We are not like the apostles Paul and Peter, who were far more skilled in battle. In comparison, we are naïve and have but little experience with the armor.

We must remember that our children are targets also. Satan wishes to sideline the soldiers of God by either a fatal blow to them or members of their family. I think we need to face the fact that our comprehension of the dangers we face is poor. Perhaps the best way to measure our preparedness is to examine our prayer life. The degree of our awareness is measured by the level of desperation poured out before the throne of grace. I write this to all who are praying and laboring in this battlefield in hope that God will use it to remind us all to pray while believing that God is with us. The Apostle Paul said, *"If God be for us, who can be against us?"(Romans 8:31).* We are on God's side but we must call upon Him and take refuge under His wings. As long as we do this, we can walk on the water and kill Goliath with a single stone. But we must remain on the alert at all times knowing that the forces of Satan are all around us.

Satan's attacks are multi-dimensional. Some of it will come from the world in the form of mocking, insults and even more aggressive persecution. Some of it may come from specific cultural groups. To prepare for these, you must resign yourself to a life of rejection. But the tactic Satan uses that catches most of us by surprise is that which comes from within the church. You need to be aware of the fact that when you set yourself to aggressively advance God's Kingdom, Satan will often use people from your own church or other churches to discourage you. For example, if you practice the things taught in this book, some will say that you paint an unloving picture of God. Some people will distance themselves from you. Beyond this, Satan will incite some Christians to mistreat you. When Christians mistreat us, greater hurt is inflicted because they are supposed to be on our side. This can cause great discouragement and confusion. So, when things seem to get very confusing, just remember who is behind it all. This way, you will be able to pray, "Forgive them for they know not what they do."

Note: For more information about how to arm yourself for opposition, see my book, **Overcoming the Power of Darkness, Using God's Spiritual Armor** described in the **Other Books by Tom Bear** section near the back of this book.

Resign yourself to a life of rejection.

I have heard many Christians say that the main reason they evangelize so rarely is because of fear. It is possible for a Christian to be afraid that they will simply fail to explain the gospel correctly. This is quite common because most of us do not consider ourselves experts at articulating our thoughts. This fear can be very useful, however, because as God told Moses, He is able to help us speak (Exodus 4:11-12). It is to our advantage that we lack confidence in our own ability to articulate the gospel in order that we seek God's power to do so. This pleases Him and makes provision for His power and glory to be displayed to us in our weakness.

But what if a person fails to proclaim the gospel because he is ashamed of being identified with Christ? Each Christian that senses some fear to proclaim the gospel must look deep within to make sure that the fear he has is not shame from being identified with Jesus. Jesus said, *"If anyone is ashamed of me and my words, the Son of Man will be ashamed of him when He comes in his glory and in the glory of the Father and of the holy angels" (Luke 9:26).* If a man does not proclaim the gospel for fear of what others might think of him as a follower of Jesus, he has no reason to be assured of his salvation. Such a man has a heart of unbelief toward the gospel. He should desperately seek God for repentance and not think lightly of his condition. We must embrace our real identity as those that this world hates. Jesus said, ***"All men will hate you because of me"*** *(Matthew 10:22). "If the world hates you, keep in mind that it hated me first. If you belonged to the world, it would love you as its own. As it is, you do not belong to the world, but I have chosen you out of the world. That is why the world hates you. Remember the words I spoke to you: `No servant is greater than his master.'* ***If they persecuted me, they will persecute you also"*** *(John 15:18-20).*

May I speak personally with you for a moment? If you fear what others might think of you, it is time to accept the fact that **if** you truly are a Christian, this world hates you and will always hate you because it hated Jesus. You must come to the place where you are expecting to see this hate directed toward you in some degree or another. You must learn to realize that the absence of that hate being directed toward you may be evidence that you are too attached to the world or worse yet, that you don't belong to Christ.[11] Just like the disciples, you must learn to take comfort whenever you see that hate being directed toward you. *"They called the apostles in and had them flogged. Then they ordered them not to speak in the name of Jesus, and let them go. The apostles left the Sanhedrin, rejoicing because they had been counted worthy of suffering disgrace for the Name" (Acts 5:40-41).* This is your new identity in Christ. It is like a uniform that was issued to you at conversion. You must get used to wearing it.

---

[11] I do not say these things in a judgmental way. Rather, I speak from my own experience. There have been times in my Christian life when I did not sense hatred being directed toward me resulting from my godly lifestyle. There have been periods of my life during which I rarely spoke of Christ to unbelievers and my lifestyle and attitudes were very much like the unbelieving world around me. I know now, however, that during periods of my life that I more desperately sought the kingdom of God and His righteousness, I experienced more resistance and opposition directed toward me as a result of things I said and wrote. Looking back, I know that it was during times that I most desperately sought after God that I found myself speaking more about gospel truth with people. Also, I have noticed a direct correlation between the amount I speak and write about Jesus and the amount of resistance, opposition and hatred that is directed toward me. If you have not been experiencing much opposition or anger being directed toward you, I recommend that you to go door–to-door in a typical American neighborhood proclaiming the gospel. Or, proclaim it more aggressively with your friends and relatives.

Know the reason the world hates us.

"To what can I compare this generation? They are like children sitting in the marketplaces and calling out to others:

'We played the flute for you, and you did not dance;
we sang a dirge, and you did not mourn.'" (Matthew 11:16-18)

Jesus had said many things to show that in this age, before He returns again, the world will hate us. In this passage, Jesus calls attention to the source of hatred that the world has toward true disciples of His. The world dances to its own tune and that tune is at enmity against God. God has been cast out of their hearts because people do not want Him interfering with or ruling over their lives. The world expects everyone to dance to this tune so that the harmony is not broken. If a person begins dancing to a different tune, the world takes note and begins to show its disapproval, both for that one and the ones who taught him how to dance to the new tune. In the case of righteous John the Baptist and Jesus, the world made false accusations to malign their character and discredit their message. They were not dancing to the tune of this world and it bothered the people of the world. It made them feel uncomfortable. What were Jesus and John saying that would cause this to happen?

The message of John the Baptist, Jesus and the rest of the apostles was one of repentance. The things they were saying called attention to the fact that the world was dancing to a tune that displeased God. It showed that the people were living lives at enmity toward God.

Before saying these words (Matthew 11:16-18), Jesus had provided some instruction to the disciples to prepare them before sending them out. Much of this instruction is found in Matthew 10:17-42. He wanted them to go prepared, knowing that they would face opposition by the world because of the message he commanded them to preach. Jesus warned them that this message would be received by some and rejected by many. He told them to simply move on when the message was rejected and look for those who are "worthy" of the message- those who receive it. Then He said that as a result of this message, lives will be changed and people will start dancing to a different tune that is in contrast to the world. He said that, because of this, the world will show its disapproval by hating and persecuting those who receive the message. The message and lives of those who receive it calls into question the way of thinking and living of the people of the world.

If we are preaching the same gospel as Jesus and the apostles, the world will not like us. It is a message that is completely incompatible with the way the world lives. If we are not sensing this hatred as individuals, then either we are not proclaiming the same gospel clearly or we are simply not speaking up at all. Let me close this section by suggesting that you read and meditate on Matthew 10:17-42.

Be prepared for cultural clashes.

During the summer of 2008, an evangelical group of singers were putting on concerts in some of the parks located in areas in which high concentrations of Muslims live. We had been going door-to-door for a few years prior to this without incident but something happened during one of those concerts that had an impact on the entire Muslim community. Some of the Muslim leaders tried to keep their people from listening to the music and the gospel message. They also confronted one of the gospel preachers to voice their displeasure. There was no violent outbreak. But after that, the leaders of several Mosques got together to discuss the situation and develop a plan of action.

We learned later that they planned to wage some sort of protest at one of the follow up concerts but it was rained out. Subsequent to these events, we noticed a marked change in the reception Muslims were giving to us as we went door-to-door. We found out from some of the people that the leaders had instructed the people that if Christians come to their door, they were supposed to direct us to the Mosque. They also were being much more protective of their children. The leaders had been instructing them to keep their children from entering into conversations with us. This particular subculture is well organized. They instructed the people as to how they should deal with us. Out of fear instilled by the leaders, many people simply do not answer the door.

I write all this to alert you to the fact that Satan uses human forces to confuse and oppose the work in many ways. Our greatest weapon is prayer because spiritual forces are behind the human forces. Whether they are incidents like the ones described here, or outright violent opposition like that going on in many parts of the world today, prayer is absolutely necessary. Unless God keeps us and protects us, we will fail. He is our fortress so let us run to Him for shelter.

Section 4: Pray or forget it!

Pray without ceasing!

Someone might think that I do not consider prayer that important because it is in the last section of the book. So let me state from the outset that unless prayer is a part of your evangelism, you will fail. Jesus said, *"Apart from me, you can do nothing"(John 15:5).* This is directly applicable to the work of evangelism. God is the One who saves. He is the One who gives boldness and utterance. He is the One to keep us from falling headlong into the most putrid sin. He is the One who protects us from satanic attack. I reserved this section for last because it gives me an opportunity to point back to all that is written previously. The realities described in this book should cause any serious-minded reader to see the great need for praying. We are called to a task that is impossible for us to do. When we engage in the advancement of God's Kingdom, we are placing ourselves smack in the middle of a great celestial battle. The Bible has already made known the ultimate Victor. But what fools are we if we march forward without His direction, His strength, His weaponry, and His presence?

Jesus said that if we ask anything according to His will, He will give it. Let me rehearse with you some things that are according to His will so you can pray confidently. Jesus taught us to pray, *"Thy Kingdom come."* In keeping with this, we can confidently ask that He advance His Kingdom in us and through us. We can pray that He will sharpen the gospel in our mouths and the mouths of His people throughout the world. We can pray that He sends revival to all of us so that our hearts will be full of love, compassion and zeal. We also can pray that God would send forth more laborers into the harvest. Do you have a close friend that shares your burden for proclaiming the gospel? You need to have such a friend, or better yet several, who will pray with you and work with you to advance God's Kingdom as a fellow soldier. If you have not done so, why not ask God for one or more friends like this?

According to Peter, we are all priests (I Peter 2:9). A major role of a priest is to intercede for people. We should have the outlook of Samuel who said, *"Far be it from me that I should sin against the LORD by failing to pray for you"(I Samuel 12:23).* Has God laid a heavy burden for a specific unbelieving person upon your heart? Exercise love and compassion by interceding for that person before the throne of grace. Share your burdens with other Christians and ask them to pray for the people God has brought across your path.

Conclusion

Jesus commissioned you and me to go and make disciples. Since this task requires the supernatural power of God to complete, we must be careful to follow God's instructions rather than make up our own methods to accomplish it. We have examined the New Testament and observed how Jesus and His disciples made new disciples. We have considered actual letters that they wrote to convey their message and considered Luke's testimony concerning the subjects the disciples discussed in their efforts to make disciples.

Based upon these observations, we learned how Jesus and his disciples made much of the sinfulness of men, the righteousness of God and the judgment to come in order to prepare hearts to receive the good news of the gospel, and how this biblical approach is applicable to people of every culture and belief system. We learned that they did not rely upon extra-biblical arguments to prove the existence of God, authority of the Bible or deity of Christ. Rather, they taught the gospel message simply on the basis that all these things are true. We have demonstrated that rather than first developing friendships, Jesus and his disciples spoke the gospel message wherever they went as they sought to make disciples.

We were reminded that we are all called to be "God's prophets" and as such must accept the fact that we will be hated by the world for who we are and what we say. We learned that by having full confidence in God's calling upon us and by having the highest regard for the gospel, we need not argue with people, and in fact we must withhold the gospel from those who make light of it. We learned that it is our responsibility to help people see their true condition before God and His demand of absolute surrender resulting from true faith and repentance in order to be reconciled to God. Finally, we learned that part of our responsibility is to baptize new disciples and guide them so that they become knit to other believers who are united to follow Christ and work in His harvest.

God has graciously made us ambassadors of Christ and co-laborers together in the harvest. He has made His message known and has given us human examples to follow. This task is impossible for us to accomplish but with God, all things are possible. He takes delight in pouring out His grace on those who desire to take up this work. We can be confident that He will cause fruit to come forth because Jesus shed His own blood to make it all possible. While each Christian is assigned different roles in the expansion of the Kingdom, we are all called to be witnesses unto Him to the uttermost parts of the world. Let us therefore cast off all encumbrances and build the Temple, knowing that the gates of hell cannot stand against it.

"If you call yourself a Christian, where are your works of love? Have you abounded, and do you abound in them? If this divine and holy principle is in you, and reigns in you, will it not appear in your life in works of love? Consider, what deeds of love have you done? Do you love God? What have you done for Him, for His glory, for the advancement of His Kingdom in the world? And how much have you denied yourself to promote the Redeemer's interest among men? Do you love your fellow-men? What have you done for them? Consider your former defects in these respects, and how becoming it is in you, as a Christian, hereafter to abound more in deeds of love. Do not make excuse that you have not opportunities to do anything for the glory of God, for the interest of the Redeemer's Kingdom, and for the spiritual benefit of your neighbors. If your heart is full of love, it will find vent; you will find and make ways enough to express your love in deeds. When a fountain abounds in water, it will send forth streams. Consider that as a principle of love is the main principle in the heart of a real Christian, so the labor of love is the main business of the Christian life."[12]

---

[12] Edwards, Jonathan, Charity and its Fruits, The Banner of Truth Trust, Carlisle, PA, 2000. p. 24 & 25

Appendixes

A: Try Exalting Christ through Door-to-door Evangelism!
B: What does it mean to "Call upon the Lord?"
C: Integrating New Believers into Local Churches
D: Use the Book of Romans to Present the Gospel to Unbelievers
E: Using tracts and gospel literature
F. Team evangelism etiquette
G. Actual Documented Gospel Conversations
H. It's better to say "remission" (of sins) than "forgiveness" (of sins)

Appendix A: Try Exalting Christ through Door-to-Door Evangelism!

(My personal challenge to you)

While doing door-to-door evangelism one Saturday, a man who professed to be a Christian came to the door and proceeded to scold me about going door-to-door. He said that it was not something God wants us to do. In 2006, a friend of mine went to a missions/evangelism conference as a regional representative of his denomination. One of the workshops he attended taught that door-to-door evangelism does not work. This was being taught as if it was a commonly accepted fact. I wish that Christians who believe this could go door-to-door with me once so they could learn the truth about door-to-door evangelism. Any true Christian that could witness one of the extended gospel conversations I have enjoyed while going door-to-door would view door-to-door evangelism as God's wide open door of opportunity to spread the gospel. I am convinced that Satan has deceived millions of Christians into thinking negatively about door-to-door evangelism. After all, he hates it when the cross is proclaimed. To deceive Christians into thinking negatively about door-to-door evangelism is a strategic means to accomplish his goal to keep the blinders on the unbelievers so that they do not see the light of Jesus.

The gospel is most efficiently conveyed one-on-one, face-to-face. When the gospel is proclaimed in larger group settings, the people listen, but only with varying degrees of attentiveness. In this type of setting, the unbeliever can more easily tune out the preacher intentionally or be distracted and thus miss much of what is being said. When we talk face-to-face with an unbeliever, he is a captive audience. In one-on-one conversations, both parties involved must listen and comprehend what the other is saying or the conversation essentially comes to a halt. As a result, each person concentrates on what the other person is saying so that he will be able to answer or ask a question or share something relevant to the statement just heard. In face-to-face conversations, we can also see the body language and facial expressions of the person with whom we are talking. We can judge better if the gospel message is getting through because it produces reaction in the hearer. Face-to-face conversations are clearly the most effective way to convey the gospel. Face-to-face conversations can take place at work, in our friend's house, at the neighborhood park, and they can also take place if you go door-to-door.

If you are a Christian, what is the real reason why you have not gone or do not go door-to-door to proclaim the gospel? Is it because you do not think you are an effective communicator of the gospel? Is it because you think it is rude to call people away from their television sets to the door? Is it because you are ashamed of Jesus? Is it because the people might think you are a Jehovah's Witness or Mormon? (Now that's a scary thought!) By chance, are you closing your ears to God's prompting? Do you realize that none of these reasons hold up in light of the cross? I am not writing this to make anyone feel guilty. I do not think that is my role. All who have been close to me over the last twenty years can attest to the fact that I am in no position to ever look down on any Christian or any unbeliever as if I am not guilty of the worst, outright wretched behavior and attitudes. Except it be for Jesus' work and grip, I would surely drift off into a thoroughly wicked existence in a moment. Please believe me that I do not want this document to produce guilt in the hearer. My goal here is to exhort and encourage believers to consider the reality that God has called us all to be witnesses unto Christ and that one way to do that very effectively and with purpose is by going door-to-door.

When I go door-to-door, I am sometimes asked if I am a Jehovah's Witness. Do you see how tragic this is? It should be the other way around. When Jehovah's Witnesses go door-to-door, people should be assuming that they are Christians coming to the door. There are less than three million Jehovah's Witnesses in the world. The Jehovah's Witnesses are virtually nonexistent when compared to the number of people who profess to know Christ. Since Christians so greatly outnumber Jehovah's Witnesses, why should they be the ones with the reputation for going door-to-door? This is pathetic! We should be ashamed of ourselves! The Jehovah's Witnesses go door-to-door as a means to gain credit with God. On the contrary, we **don't** go door-to-door to earn credits with God. Our motivation is simply to tell people about the wonder we see in Jesus. Do we see His glory or not? Is He awesome or not? Going door-to-door is legal in the United States, though this may soon change.[13] Millions of Christians should be going door-to-door every day to proclaim the excellencies of Jesus. The fact that it is not happening is absurd. Wouldn't it be great if when we go up to a door, the people assume that Christians are the ones knocking? We Christians have absolutely no excuse why each house in this country is not visited at least once each year by Christians going door-to-door. If you don't see it this way, please write me to explain why not. I am curious to know.

*"If anyone would come after me, he **must** deny himself and take up his cross daily and follow me. For whoever wants to save his life will lose it, but whoever loses his life for me will save it. What good is it for a man to gain the whole world, and yet lose or forfeit his very self? If anyone is ashamed of me and my words, the Son of Man will be ashamed of him when he comes in his glory and in the glory of the Father and of the holy angels" (Luke 9:23-26).*

---

[13] If your city has an ordinance against evangelizing door to door, it is unconstitutional and should be challenged in court. The Supreme Court settled this several years ago.

Appendix B: What does it mean to "Call upon the Lord?"

"Whoever calls on the name of the LORD shall be saved" (Romans 10:13).

Preface note for this appendix:

God is at work motivating His people throughout the world to fulfill the Great Commission. We praise Him for this! Many books have been written to inspire and teach Christians how to evangelize. Styles and techniques vary. Some of these practices are fruitful and biblical. But there are millions of Christians employing techniques that are not biblical and in fact, detrimental. This appendix takes aim at one of those practices.

Someone might ask if it is appropriate for me to criticize how other people evangelize. As I begin, I want to answer this question. It is always right for me or any Christian to call attention to something that is wrong. Believers are to reverence God. One clear way to do this is to pay close attention to what He has said. If we are doing things that undermine what He has said, we must stop doing it. Otherwise, our love for Him is in question. We are not at liberty to make things up as we go!

If you are one of Christ's Ambassadors, you have a duty to represent Him in a way He wants to be represented. How can we know how He wants us to represent Him? We must closely examine[14] what He has said and follow His instructions. If we are negligent to do this, we prove ourselves unfaithful, slothful and presumptuous. This appendix calls attention to some things He has made clear. If your current evangelism practices are in harmony with the things conveyed here, great. But if not, the burden is on you to justify your practices using the Bible as your authority. You do not have a license to operate in accordance with your own pragmatic thinking if that thinking conflicts with what God has previously made clear.

---

[14] *"Be diligent to present yourself approved to God, a worker who does not need to be ashamed, rightly dividing the word of truth" (II Timothy 2:15).*

The point of this appendix

In their attempt to evangelize, many Christians instruct unbelievers to pray a "sinner's prayer" [15] in order to be "saved." By "saved," they more accurately mean being justified (remission of sins) which takes place the moment a person first believes. Often, Romans 10:13 (shown above) is used to justify this practice. It is viewed almost like a recipe.

The unbiblical recipe model:

The act		The result
One-time sinner's prayer	>	justification/remission
		("salvation")

This appendix will prove that anyone who justifies this practice on the basis of Romans 10:13 is doing so based upon a distorted view of this verse. This appendix will use both context and syntax to help the reader see exactly what the Apostle Paul was trying to communicate in this passage.

Argument based upon syntax

Because the details of this argument based upon syntax are somewhat technical, I will only make a summary here. The details may be found near the end of this appendix in the section called, **Details of the syntactical argument**.

---

[15] Such a prayer can be viewed on many tracts. The unbeliever is told to repeat a prayer that goes something like this. "God, I have sinned against you. You have given your Son Jesus to die for my sins. Jesus, I ask you now to come into my heart and save me from my sins. Amen." The people are often told that if they prayed this prayer and meant it, they are now saved from their sins and will go to heaven after they die.

By "syntax," I mean the structure of the New Testament Greek text as it relates to this subject. Sometimes, excellent clues are provided in the Greek text to help us understand more accurately what the authors were trying to communicate. There are some relevant syntax observations to consider that relate to the subject at hand but most of the case can be made from the immediate and overall **context** of the entire Bible. Put another way, most of what is relevant to this topic can be proven from the English Bible. This will be done in the section, *Argument based upon context*. But before we examine the argument based upon context, let me summarize the thrust of the argument based upon syntax.

The syntax argument rests mainly on the tense of the Greek word ἐπικαλέω (*epikaleo*-to call, invoke) when it is used in the phrase "call upon the Lord." Briefly, when using this expression (call upon the Lord), the authors never chose a verb tense that conveys a one-time act or calling or praying. In those verses that do convey tense aspect, the idea embedded in the verb is always a repeated act of calling or praying that does not cease. In other words, the Greek syntax suggests a lifestyle of praying (calling out) not a one-time act. So, the New Testament speaks of calling upon the Lord as a way of life, not a one-time prayer. For the details of this argument, see the section called, **Details of the syntactical argument** which appears near the end of this appendix.

Argument based upon context

⁹If you confess with your mouth the Lord Jesus and believe in your heart that God has raised Him from the dead, you will be saved. ¹⁰For with the heart one believes unto righteousness, and with the mouth confession is made unto salvation. ¹¹For the Scripture says, "Whoever believes on Him will not be put to shame." ¹²For there is no distinction between Jew and Greek, for the same Lord over all is rich to all who call upon Him. ¹³For "whoever calls on the name of the LORD shall be saved." ¹⁴How then shall they call on Him in whom they have not believed? And how shall they believe in Him of whom they have not heard? And how shall they hear without a preacher?" (Romans 10:9-14).

We are attempting to understand what Paul meant by the words, *"Whoever calls on the name of the Lord shall be saved"* (in verse 13 above). To support his overall argument in chapter ten, Paul directly quotes from Joel 2:32. Therefore, we must examine the Joel passage first if we stand any chance of properly understanding what Paul meant when he quoted Joel.

*"And **I will show wonders in the heavens and in the earth: Blood and fire and pillars of smoke. The sun shall be turned into darkness, And the moon into blood, Before the coming of the great and awesome day of the Lord.** And it shall come to pass That **whoever calls on the name of the Lord Shall be saved.** For in Mount Zion and in Jerusalem there shall be deliverance, As the Lord has said, Among the remnant whom the Lord calls"* (Joel 2:30-32).

The first thing we notice is that Joel was talking about being saved from God's wrath that will be poured out on the Day of Judgment. Therefore, we know that when he quoted Joel, Paul was saying that those who "call upon the Lord" will be saved from God's wrath that will be poured out on the Day of Judgment. He was not talking about justification and remission of sins that occurs when a person first believes. This point alone sufficiently proves that Romans 10:13 cannot be used to justify the practice of instructing a person to pray a sinner's prayer in order to be justified and forgiven (since Paul was talking about the salvation from God's wrath on the Day of Judgment). But this is only one minor part of my argument.

The "sinner's prayer" formula puts the cart before the horse. Notice what Paul says in verse 14 immediately after saying "whoever calls upon the Lord will be saved." *How then shall they call on Him in whom they have not believed?* Clearly, Paul says that before a person can "call upon the Lord," he must first believe, not visa versa. Verse 14 should confuse those who insist on instructing people to pray a sinner's prayer. Verse 14 shouldn't make any sense to them. But it makes clear sense to anyone who understands what the Bible means by the phrase "call upon the Lord."

Calling on the Lord is a way of living, NOT a one time "sinner's prayer!"

Abraham "called upon the Lord" often.

- *"Then the LORD appeared to Abram and said, "To your descendants I will give this land." And there he built an altar to the LORD, who had appeared to him. 8 And he moved from there to the mountain east of Bethel, and he pitched his tent with Bethel on the west and Ai on the east; there he built an altar to the LORD and called on the name of the LORD" (Genesis 12:7-8).*
- *"And there Abram called on the name of the LORD" (Genesis 13:4).*
- *"Abraham planted a tamarisk tree in Beersheba, and there called on the name of the LORD, the Everlasting God" (Genesis 21:33).*

These are just three instances that are recorded. In reality, Abraham called upon the Lord as a way of life because he believed God. He relied upon God and prayed all the time. This is what people of faith do. David's testimony confirms this. *"To you I call, O LORD my Rock; do not turn a deaf ear to me. For if you remain silent, I will be like those who have gone down to the pit. Hear my cry for mercy as I call to you for help, as I lift up my hands toward your Most Holy Place" (Psalm 28:1-2).* (See other examples in Psalm 50:14-15, 86:3-7, 145:18.)

The Bible is packed with testimonies of God's people "calling upon the Lord" as a way of relating to Him for life. This characteristic distinguishes believers from unbelievers. Believers live their lives in dependence on God. Unbelievers live autonomously. The New Testament record is in complete harmony with these Old Testament passages. (See I Corinthians 1:2, I Peter 1:17 and Acts 9:14 which are examined in detail in the section called, **Details of the syntactical argument** which appears later in this appendix.)

"Calling upon the Lord" is a way of relating to God for life and NOT a one-time act of a sinner asking for forgiveness. We know from Scripture that before a man believes, he is a slave to his own desires and all of life is self-directed with the aim to gratify himself. As Isaiah says, *"All we like sheep have gone astray, each of us has turned to his own way" (Isaiah 53:6a).* Paul says that we were dead in our trespasses and sins (Ephesians 2:1-2) and that no one seeks God (Romans 3:11). Thus, the natural man does not "call upon the Lord" or submit to His direction and provision. (This is why Paul said in Romans 10:14, *"How then shall they call on Him in whom they have not believed?"*)

When a person is born again and believes, there is an immediate turning (repentance) to God. Now, instead of a self-directed life, the person "calls upon the Lord" as a way of life. Instead of self-sufficiency, there is a heart-felt dependence on God for all that is necessary. This dependency on God and renunciation of self-reliance is evidence of the new nature. Without this evidence, there should be no assurance of salvation.

This appendix proves that Romans 10:13 cannot be used as a basis for instructing a person to pray a sinner's prayer. The promise, "Whoever calls upon the Lord will be saved" may not be used for this purpose! This promise may only be used to comfort true believers who call upon the Lord as a way of living. Only these people will be saved in the end from the wrath of God that will be poured out on Judgment Day!

Instructing a person to pray a sinner's prayer conflicts with the biblical record. There is not a single occurrence of anyone being instructed to pray a sinner's prayer in the Bible. The Apostles instructed people to believe the gospel from the heart in order to be justified and receive remission of sins. They instructed people who wish to follow Jesus to show their allegiance to Him by being baptized. They taught that believing was not a one-time act of accepting a set of beliefs. Rather, it was a repeating act that never stops. If it stops, it is false belief.

Why this is important?

If you tell a person that he can have confidence about heaven as a result of praying a sinner's prayer, you are giving him false assurance. Biblical hope (assurance) is not based upon the mouthing of a sinner's prayer. It is based upon a changed life full of fruits of the Holy Spirit. If the Spirit of Jesus dwells in a person, he has reason to believe that he will be saved from the wrath of God that will be poured out at the judgment. *"Christ in you, the hope of glory" (Colossians 1:27).*

Millions of people have prayed a sinner's prayer and falsely assume that they are heaven bound. Not good! After reading this appendix, I hope you realize that this is not a matter to be taken lightly. You do not want to be the one who falsely assures a person that he is heaven bound if in reality, he is still headed for hell. Please stop instructing people to pray a sinner's prayer. It is not biblical. Therefore, it is irreverent to instruct people to pray a sinner's prayer.

Details of the syntactical argument *(Observations of the Greek syntax that convey a repeated calling/praying)*

The Romans 10 Greek:

*"For whoever **calls** on the name of the LORD shall be saved" (Romans 10:13).*

Romans 10:13 πᾶς γὰρ ὃς ἂν **ἐπικαλέσηται** τὸ ὄνομα κυρίου σωθήσεται

In this verse, **ἐπικαλέσηται** (calls) appears as a subjunctive participle, aorist. Because it is in the subjunctive mood, <u>nothing</u> can be derived from this that speaks to aspect or time. So, we must expand our sampling. We don't have to look very far at all. (The prior verse.)

*"For there is no distinction between Jew and Greek, for the same Lord over all is rich to all who **call** upon Him" Romans 10:12).*

Romans 10:12 οὐ γὰρ ἔστιν διαστολὴ Ἰουδαίου τε καὶ Ἕλληνος ὁ γὰρ αὐτὸς κύριος πάντων πλουτῶν εἰς πάντας τοὺς **ἐπικαλουμένους** αὐτόν

In this verse, the verb appears as a present, participle. It is a substantival (independent) adjectival participle. Because the referents are in a narrowly defined group (those who call upon the Lord), there is good reason to consider its verbal aspect remains in force. This combination of facts conveys the Greek customary present tense. In other words, it conveys an action that repeats and never stops.

The overall New Testament Greek

Here is another Pauline example:

*"To the church of God which is at Corinth, to those who are sanctified in Christ Jesus, called to be saints, with all who in every place **call** on the name of Jesus Christ our Lord, both theirs and ours" (I Corinthians 1:2).*

1 Corinthians 1:2 τῇ ἐκκλησίᾳ τοῦ θεοῦ τῇ οὔσῃ ἐν

Κορίνθῳ ἡγιασμένοις ἐν Χριστῷ Ἰησοῦ κλητοῖς ἁγίοις σὺν πᾶσιν

τοῖς **ἐπικαλουμένοις** τὸ ὄνομα τοῦ κυρίου ἡμῶν Ἰησοῦ Χριστοῦ ἐν

παντὶ τόπῳ αὐτῶν καὶ ἡμῶ

In this verse, the verb appears as a present participle with no controlling verb. (It acts as a noun.) When acting as a noun, the participle tense remains in the indicative force. In other words, this verse also conveys an action that repeats and never stops (Greek customary present).

Here is one from Peter:

*"And if you **call on** the Father, who without partiality judges according to each one's work, conduct yourselves throughout the time of your stay here in fear" (I Peter 1:17).*

1 Peter 1:17 καὶ εἰ πατέρα **ἐπικαλεῖσθε** τὸν

ἀπροσωπολήμπτως κρίνοντα κατὰ τὸ ἑκάστου ἔργον ἐν φόβῳ τὸν

τῆς παροικίας ὑμῶν χρόνον ἀναστράφητε

In this verse, this verb appears in the indicative mood, present tense. In other words, Peter, like Paul, is conveying an action that repeats and never stops. (Greek customary present).

Here is one from Luke:

*"And here he has authority from the chief priests to bind all who **call on** Your name" (Acts 9:14).*

Acts 9:14 καὶ ὧδε ἔχει ἐξουσίαν παρὰ τῶν ἀρχιερέων δῆσαι

πάντας τοὺς **ἐπικαλουμένους** τὸ ὄνομά σου

In this verse, the verb appears as a present, participle. It is a substantival (independent) adjectival participle. Because the referents are in a narrowly defined group (those who call upon the Lord), there is good reason to consider its verbal aspect remains in force. This combination of facts conveys the Greek customary present tense. In other words, it conveys an action that repeats and never stops.

All of these samples convey an action that repeats and never stops. There are no examples (relating to the phrase "call upon the Lord") in the New Testament (or Old Testament for that matter) that convey a one-time prayer.

Conclusion of the syntactical argument

The Greek syntax used when talking about "calling upon the Lord" cannot be used to support the practice of instructing a person to repeat a "sinner's prayer" as a one-time act that results in salvation. In fact, the Greek syntax used when talking about "calling upon the Lord" consistently conveys a repeated, never ending practice. It should be noted that the New Testament Greek syntax witness is in complete harmony with the Old Testament testimony relating to this subject which is discussed in the **Argument based upon context** section of this appendix.

So what is a biblical invitation to sinners?

The biblical invitation in its simplest form is "Believe on the Lord Jesus Christ and you will be saved." And to be consistent with the rest of Scripture, I teach that this salvation is a result of a life-long believing on Jesus as evidenced by a holy life of obedience to Him. But since most people think that believing is merely an intellectual exercise, we should say some things to help them understand what happens once a person "believes from the heart." Before I was saved, I enjoyed my life and did not want anyone messing with it, including God. I had many friends and looked forward to every party. I look back now and realize that when I embraced Jesus, I lost that life I once held so dear. My life is completely different. Jesus gave me a totally new heart. I now hate those things I once loved. Before I was saved, I used to think that anything having to do with God was boring. Now, I love Him and enjoy Him. I love the things He loves and hate the things He hates. He made me into a new creature (II Corinthians 5:17).

When talking with those who seem to be considering Christ, I tell them that when a man "believes from the heart," his life will never be the same. Because he has a new heart, he will gladly surrender control of his life to God. He will joyfully give up his status as God's enemy and enjoy true peace with God forever. I often quote Jesus words, "WHOEVER WANTS TO SAVE HIS LIFE WILL LOSE IT, BUT WHOEVER LOSES HIS LIFE FOR ME WILL SAVE IT" (LUKE 9:24). I tell people that any man who truly "believes from the heart," is willing to die for Jesus and suffer for His name's sake.

To be saved, a person must simply believe the gospel "from the heart." We can ask the person if they truly believe the gospel "from the heart." If he says, "Yes," we can then ask him if he believes that God will accept him into heaven. If his answer to this question is, "No," then we need to go back over the gospel with him. If his answer is, "Yes," we can ask him why he thinks God will accept him into heaven. If he believes the gospel "from the heart," he will say something that conveys the idea that he will be accepted by God into heaven <u>because Jesus took his punishment and God has promised to receive all who come to Him through Jesus</u>. We should invite people like this to be baptized as a means for them to declare their allegiance to Christ. If we live in a country where there is danger of being killed after being baptized in the name of Jesus, their declaration will demonstrate all the more that they "believe from the heart."

In summary, to have a person "pray to receive Christ" is leading them down a path that could be met with peril. There are many people that falsely think they are Christians just because they prayed a "sinner's prayer." We must be careful to stick to the scriptural model that exhorts people to simply believe the gospel from the heart. When they believe the gospel from the heart, they will be justified and they will be new creatures that begin to live a life that is characterized by "calling on the Lord." And only if they continue to call upon the Lord as a way of living until they die will they be saved from the wrath of God that is coming upon the earth at the final judgment.

Appendix C: Integrating New Believers into Local Churches

If God used you in bringing a person to new life in Christ, you are the one who will be the most concerned for his spiritual growth and wellbeing. You should take responsibility to make sure he is cared for properly. While God can and will use other Christians to help in this matter, you should be the primary spiritual care giver for this new believer. You need to make sure he is integrated into a local church, preferably your own. We might recommend to a new believer from the neighborhood where our church meets that he begins to fellowship at our church. Depending on the circumstances, it may be best to start a new church with the support of the church you have been attending. We must be open to what God might want specifically for each particular new convert. For example, what if the new believer is from a completely different culture and what if English is his second language? What if a church does not exist near the new believer? Is it essential that the new Christian begins visiting a large building? Should we insist that he become a part of our church if it is not prepared to care properly for him?

We must remember that God always has a solution that is in accordance with biblical teaching and strive to keep our minds clear of all the extra-biblical practices that might be associated with churches of our culture. God may want the new believer from another culture to begin fellowshipping with other new believers from that same culture, meeting in houses rather than a church building.

Since it is God who is most passionate about the building of His Church, we should look to Him for guidance and do our best to avoid contaminating new believers with our preconceived ideas and cultural trappings. In cross-cultural situations, God raises up new bodies of believers that worship Him in ways that may appear different in some respects to our own ways. Rather than impose our ways and think of this new Body of believers as a subset of "our church," we should probably consider it "their church" and merely seek to serve them and offer guidance that will insure adherence to sound biblical doctrine. While this book is not intended to answer all the questions that relate to this matter, it is important that we remember that when disciples are made, they must become united to the Body of Christ (His Church) and that God's plan for the new disciples may be much different than what we had in mind. We must seek His direction for every situation.

If you are involved in evangelism, remember that when the gospel is proclaimed, new disciples are eventually made. You should give thought to these things before that occurs so you know what to do when God decides to bless you with new disciples. You should consider whether a new church should be planted and if so, what it should be like. To help you think this through, I recommend my book, **The Local Church** which is described in **the Other Books by Tom Bear** section near the back of this book.

Appendix D: Use the Book of Romans to Present the Gospel

The following verses from Romans, along with a brief notation relating to each one, may be used to present the gospel to an unbeliever. With a Bible open before the unbeliever, you can start by turning to Romans 1:20 and asking him to read each verse slowly or read it out loud for him as he reads along silently. Then you can ask him what he observes from reading the verse and point out gospel truth to him as noted below for each verse. Progress through Romans in the order the verses appear ending up with Romans 10:9 & 10. If the person comprehends what was discussed, he will have gained an intellectual understanding of the gospel.

Romans 1:20: God created all things and therefore, all people are accountable to serve and honor Him as Lord over all creation and their lives. (See also Revelation 4:11 & Genesis 1:1)

Romans 3:11: Absolutely nobody "seeks God" or lets Him have complete rule over them. (See also Isaiah 53:6a)

Romans 3:12: There is absolutely nobody that qualifies as "good" in God's sight.

Romans 3:13: All people are liars by nature.

Romans 3:15: Murderous thoughts and feelings often occupy the hearts of all people. (See also Mark 7:21)

Romans 3:19 & 20: All people are accountable to God for their actions and deserve punishment for their sins of rebellion against God. It is impossible to make up for our sins by trying to do acts of righteousness. (also Isaiah 64:6)

Romans 5:6 & 8 and 6:23: Though we deserve eternal punishment, God made a way for someone else (Jesus) to take our punishment and satisfy His righteous demand for justice.

Romans 10:9 & 10: If any man believes "from the heart" that he deserves eternal death/punishment (earlier verses) but that Jesus took that punishment for him and then was raised from the dead, he will be saved. If he truly believes from the heart, he will identify himself with Jesus even if his life is being threatened for doing so and he will gladly relate to Jesus as the new loving ruler over his life.

Romans 12:1: To offer yourself to God, you must first agree that though you use to rule your life, God is your new loving ruler. He has the right to do whatever He wants with your life from now on.

Suggestion: You might consider highlighting these verses with a unique color so that you can simply open your Bible to Romans and step through each verse in the order they appear in the book. This will automatically keep you organized so that the gospel is discussed in a logical order. A color highlighter is recommended to make each discussion verse stand out better. It might also be helpful to write in the margin (next to each of the Romans passages) key words that will help you remember points to make about that passage. For example, next to Romans 3:19 and 20, you might write, *"Accountable, No excuses, Judgment deserved"* and another note, *"Good deeds can't make up for our debt of sin (Isaiah 64:6)"*.

Appendix E: Using tracts and gospel literature

I consider mass tract distribution to be a form of gospel proclamation. By its nature, it is far less proficient than proclaiming the gospel to a person face-to-face. Many tracts, once received, are thrown in the trash. Many of them are read casually rather than carefully. Nevertheless, some people have come to faith in Christ after reading a tract that was handed to them. I would never oppose the mass distribution of good, gospel-centered tracts. I would like to suggest, however, that if a man only passes out tracts and never engages in two-way gospel conversations, he is an inefficient evangelist because he is relying on an inefficient means to proclaim the gospel. I would encourage such a man, unless he cannot speak, to apply himself to learn how to proclaim the gospel with his mouth in order to make the best use of his time and so that he has opportunity to more likely and more often see Christ exalted as he watches people hear the gospel and believe.

I believe that the most appropriate use of tracts is to supplement face-to-face gospel proclamation. If the conversation includes dialog about sin, righteousness and judgment, then the tract or gospel will more likely be a valued, useful reference after the evangelist leaves. Even if the conversation gets cut short, the tract is more meaningful because it was given to him in a more personal way. The person is more likely to read and consider it.

When selecting tracts, do so considering how the tract will be used. If it is going to be mass distributed, then a more attractive tract will be more efficient. But if you plan to use the tract as a supplement to gospel conversations, then it can be printed on normal printer paper since it will be used primarily as a summary of the gospel conversation. The tract you hand out should be one that adequately conveys the message of redemption in Christ. If there are words in it that add to or distort the gospel, such as a "sinner's prayer," then find a different tract. If the tract does not adequately address the matters of sin, righteousness and judgment, then look for another one. The tract should represent the redemption message that you proclaim and want the person to know. If you cannot find good tracts, then write your own tracts. If desired, you can obtain free tracts in PDF format from the Stones Cry Out Ministries web site that can be personalized with your own contact information. (**www.StonesCryOut.INFO**)

Appendix F: Team evangelism etiquette

If more than one Christian speaks at the same time during a gospel conversation, chaos results and progress with the gospel will cease. I suggest that team members decide which person will be leading the discussion prior to starting any conversation. It is important that the other member remains silent while the leader is talking. He should try not to interrupt the leader of that conversation.

During a gospel conversation, the one listening will likely think of truth that would be good to communicate. But the leader is the one directing the conversation and this requires a great deal of concentration on his part. Interruptions often change the direction of the conversation and this makes it difficult for the leader to reign it back in and pick up where he left off. Yet, there may be something that the leader may have overlooked that is important. If so, the silent member should wait until the leader seems to be coming to a pause in the conversation before asking if he can make a statement. The statement should not be off the subject. It should be something that is germane to the points that the leader has been making. One great way to support the leader is to look up Bible passages that support what he is saying. When appropriate, the silent member can ask if he can read a passage that illustrates the leader's point.

Appendix G: Actual Documented Gospel Conversations

As a practice, I document the noteworthy gospel conversations I have with the people I meet. Most of the people I meet happen to be Muslim but the principles described in this book apply to people from any culture. When I do meet an atheist or someone from an eastern religion, I might say a couple of things differently in the beginning of the conversation just to get things started. But the general content of the overall conversation remains pretty consistent from one person to the next.

A few of my gospel conversations appear in this Appendix to help you see how I apply the principles I have written about in this book. (I publish these conversations via email to people who pray. Normally, these include specific prayer requests. Because the purpose for providing these conversations here, I stripped out the prayer requests.) Just FYI, these conversations were not recorded. I write these things from memory. Therefore, what appears below does not contain every single thing spoken during the conversations. These records contain abbreviations. GOJ means Gospel of John, GOJ/R means Gospel of John and Romans combined.

Hamid: Iranian Muslim man in his 20's. As we were walking towards the first house on our target route, we met Hamid who was standing near his car. We learned that he was with a company that builds houses and he was observing the digging of a basement. We talked a few minutes about the nature of his work. Then, I told him that we were Christians going door to door to talk with people about the way to heaven. I asked him if he had interest to talk with us and his response indicated that perhaps God was at work drawing his attention to the gospel.

I told him that I wanted to talk about a subject that many Christians seem unwilling to discuss...the judgment of God. I told him that because so few Christians talk about it, he will probably learn something he has never known before as a result of our discussion.

I said, "Since you are a Muslim, you believe that God is a God of justice, right?" He agreed. Then I said that the Bible portrays God's justice differently than the koran portrays it. I told him that the Bible portrays it as very strict, absolute.

To illustrate I said, "According to the Bible, if you lived your entire life without sinning except for one little lie and then died with just that one little lie on your account, God would have no choice but to send you to hell forever." He was surprised at my statement. I said, "Seems strict right?" He agreed. I said that while the Bible teaches that God is rich in mercy, His justice is absolute so He must punish all sin. Otherwise, He would cease to be righteous.

I told him that from the beginning, God has been telling the people that He requires a sacrifice for sins. I quoted, "Without the shedding of blood, there can be no remission of sins." I explained the animal sacrifices and told him that these taught about the need for a sacrifice but they could never take away sins. I then explained the Passover story to him. He liked learning about it. He told us he had heard about the Jewish Passover but never understood it before. He understood the idea of the lamb dying so that the people would be spared. (Substitution).

I then said that the prophets long before Jesus spoke about a Messiah who would come from God for the purpose of being the perfect sacrifice for sins. He would be without sin, a perfect lamb. I told him that on the night He was betrayed, Jesus was with his friends observing the Passover feast but He made it all about Him. He took the bread, broke it and said, "This is my body which is broken for you, from now on, when you do this (feast), do it in remembrance of me." He did likewise with the cup. I told him that entire Bible is all about what Jesus did by dying as a sacrifice lamb in our behalf. All of these images were causing Hamid to suddenly understand the gospel. He then restated everything we told him as if it was all making perfect sense to him.

I said that there is another thing he must know. I told him that many Muslims respond by saying, "This is convenient for you Christians. Since Jesus paid for your sins, you can live any way you like." Hamid frowned as if he knew this was inappropriate. But I took the time to explain regeneration to him to demonstrate that if a person truly believes the gospel, they believe all things that God has spoken in His word. For example, they come to Jesus believing that He is Lord of all. They happily relate to him as if He is King and they are his lowly servants. I then said that this is because God changes them inside making them into totally new people. He puts His Spirit inside of them to live. Their desires change. They now see sin as horrific and they desire to please God.

I said, "People like us do the things that please God, not to become accepted into heaven. Jesus already paid for that. We do so because we enjoy pleasing God. We have been born again. I told him that all people are born slaves to sin and unable to achieve righteousness that God requires. I told him that he is a slave to sin and is unable to achieve righteousness in his own power. But we are no longer slaves to sin. All who truly believe the gospel of Jesus Christ are being conformed to the same life type as Jesus.

Hamid raised a few questions as we progressed. For example, he asked about people that lived before Jesus. I explained that the sacrifice of Jesus applies to all people that believed what God said. I explained how Abraham believed the things God told him, including the promise that a man would descend from Abraham through whom all nations would be blessed. But Jesus is the lamb of God slain from the foundation of the world. He understood this idea very well.

He also asked about people who never heard any of this. I explained that God has spoken to all men through creation and as a result, they are accountable to Him to live obedient lives. But they don't care at all about God as Lord. They are all, like everyone else, fully deserving of hell. But then I told him that he is different from those people in that he has now heard the message and understood it.

I said that we consider this all to be good news because we believe we deserve hell but Jesus made a way of escape. We consider it a supreme act of love. Hamid nodded in agreement. Then I told him that he cannot have any of the benefit of what Jesus offers unless he first acknowledges that Jesus died, and that He died personally for his sins. I paused to let that sink in. I could tell from his facial expression that he understood because he had a slight frown on his face.

I gave him a tract and offered him a gospel. But he told us a girl gave him a Bible so he took the tract only. Hamid thanked us and told us he enjoyed learning what we told him. He lives in Ann Arbor which is too far for us to follow up with him. Normally, going door to door, we get their contact information since we are standing right on their porch. But we gave Hamid our contact information and asked him to contact us if he has more questions. He said he planned to read our tract carefully.

David, Roman Catholic young man in his early 20's. He told us that he had not been to church for a while because he is so busy. But he seemed willing to listen to us. I said, "If you were to die tonight and stand before God and He asked you why He should let you into heaven, what would you say?" He paused and said that he thinks it is because of forgiveness. I told him his answer was a little better than many we hear but how is it possible for God to provide forgiveness? The Bible teaches that God is righteous and will not let the guilty go unpunished. David did not seem to have an answer.

Perhaps he felt unsure of his answers because we were putting him on the spot. So, told him the answer as something he has heard before. I said, "Have you heard the phrase, 'Jesus died for our sins?'" He said yes. I said that this is the only way that God could ever provide forgiveness. The sins had to be punished. If you die in your sins, you will have to take the full punishment for your sins in hell forever. But God made a way of salvation. Jesus lovingly took your punishment. All who believe this in their hearts receive remission of sins and eternal life.

I then told him that to us, we find this to be wonderful. We believe that we fully deserve to go to hell for our sins. So, we are very grateful. But judging your expressions and response, it seems like you may not feel all that grateful for what Jesus did by dying for you on the cross. If my assessment is true, then perhaps you really do not believe the gospel in your heart. Jesus said that all who truly believe the gospel are very grateful.

Jesus also said that unless a man loses his life, he will not find it. All who are truly his disciples gladly surrender their lives to Jesus. He said, "Unless a man is born again, he cannot see the kingdom of heaven." This is what happened to us many years ago. Could it be that you have not been born again? God has made us alive in Christ. He has put His Spirit in us. Before, we lived lives for ourselves and we were the boss over them. But now, because He made us alive in Christ, we do the things that please Him. We do not do it to get into heaven. Jesus already paid for that. We do it because we love him and enjoy pleasing Him.

I told David that I hope God uses our meeting to bother him and make him consider seriously the gospel. I handed him the "Who Runs Your Life?" tract and said that to me, it appears that David is the one running his life and if he dies living this way, he will go to hell forever. I said that Jesus wants David's life and if David begins to follow Jesus and loses his life to Him, He will not be disappointed. We also told him to try reading one of the gospels. We plan to visit him again.

Hyat: Lebanese woman in her 50's. After introducing ourselves, we asked if she wanted to talk with us about the way to heaven. She agreed and asked us to sit on her porch with her. After a little small talk, I explained the righteousness of God to her.

She has been speaking English for 7 years but she was obviously struggling at times to understand. It seemed that she was doubting her ability to understand us because the things we were saying were not things she was expecting us to say. She wanted to think that she was on the same page with us and listened looking for common ground. So, when we said that every single sin must be punished and that the correct punishment is hell forever, she chimed in as if she agreed. So, we had to go over these things for almost an hour and even then, it was unclear that she was feeling the full weight of what she was hearing.

Nevertheless, it seemed as if she wanted to hear and understand. We eventually explained how Jesus came here exactly because of our need to be saved. We all stood condemned because of our sin but He came to take our punishment. And, like many Muslims, she piped up with the fact that they do not believe that Jesus died. So, again, we explained that this is what all of the prophets talked about...a messiah who would come here to die so that we might be saved. This is what the entire Bible is all about.

We explained the animal sacrifices. We explained the account with Abraham and his son and also the Passover to show that God requires a sacrifice. The lamb dies so that we might be spared the punishment. We warned her that unless she changes her mind about Jesus dying, she will go to the judgment and have to take the punishment for her sins and it will be hell forever with no escape.

During the conversation, she would occasionally ask a question that was sincere. For example, she brought up the R.C. practice of going to confession. We explained that this was not biblical, but a man-made practice that denies the fact that Jesus is our "go between." During the process of explaining all this, the subject of how Christians deal with sin came up. We again explained that the basis is completely different than the Muslim experience for many reasons.

First, all of our sin has been washed from us and God now looks upon us with favor as his children. Jesus bore all our sin and took the wrath of God that we deserved. In contrast, the wrath of God abides upon all Muslims because they stand condemned because of their sin before God. But the blood of Jesus cleanses us (the true Christians) from all unrighteousness.

Second, all true Christians have been born again. As a result, they are no longer slaves to sin. But all Muslims are slaves to sin and do not have the power to live holy lives. All they can do is try to live in a way that appears righteous. But inside, they are corrupt and cannot free themselves from sin's bondage.

Linda (my wife) then testified how God made us into new creatures. Hyat seemed most intrigued by the actual testimony that shined the light on Jesus' ability to save us from the slavery to sin. I chimed in by saying, "Now, we do the things that please God, not in order to get to heaven because Jesus paid for that in our behalf. But we do it because we enjoy it!" We all testified how God has made us alive to him.

Suddenly, the next door neighbor asked Hyat if everything was okay. She told us later that she was Episcopalian. I suspect that she thought we may have been J.W.'s and wanted to come to the aid of her neighbor. She eventually came over with that intention. We told her that we were protestant evangelicals. I think that she was still not satisfied. Based upon her countenance, it seems that if we had come to her door, she would have told us to go away. (But I cannot know this for sure.) We tried to be very polite and did not want to appear argumentative with a fellow protestant in front of Hyat.

We learned that this neighbor was about to go to Canada to visit relatives. I told her that all my relatives were from Canada and that some of them lived in Guelph, Ontario. She said that that is where she was headed today. She seemed to become more comfortable with us after that. Then she left. I did not want her to come back later and bad mouth us or our message. We only left an Arabic tract so she (the neighbor) won't be able to find out our message very well to bad mouth it. (We don't know for sure she would do this but you never know.)

Hyat invited us to come back and talk more. There were times that her smile gave way to a look of seriousness so it seems that some of the implications of the gospel were getting through.

Hassan, 18 year old Muslim boy. We first asked if his father was home but he said that the entire family was away for a short vacation. After we asked if he would be interested in talking about the way to heaven, he told us he is interested in it. I told him that we would say things that he probably has not heard about before.

I said that most of what we have to say involves the justice of God. I said that the Bible teaches things about God's justice that are much different than Islam's teachings. I told him I would make a statement to illustrate. I said, "If you were to live your entire life without sinning except for telling on little lie and then go to the judgment with that one little lie, God would have no choice but to send you to hell forever." He said, "Really?" By his response, I knew he was actually listening.

For the next few minutes I elaborated on this subject until he understood that God's righteousness is absolute. I also told him the analogy of the human judge who fails to uphold justice by letting a murderer go free simply because the murderer had remorse. I explained that God is not like that human judge. He cannot simply excuse sin just because a person feels remorse. He must punish each and every sin and the correct punishment is hell forever because our sins are much more serious than we can imagine.

I then asked him if he ever heard the stories about Musa (Moses). He said, "The man with the stick?" I said yes. He then asked, "Does your book talk about Musa?" I took out my Bible and held the O.T. portion separately and said, "All this contains the Jew's sacred writings. The beginning of it is "the book of Musa." But all the prophets are in here such as Dawoud (David) Ibraheme (Abraham), Nua (Noah). I then said that the rest of it are the writings mainly of Jesus' disciples that Muslims might refer to as Injil. He told us that he never knew this before and was almost amazed by it.

Getting back to Moses, I asked if he knew the story of God judging Egypt. I rehearsed some of it and he remembered. I then told him about the last plague, the killing of the first born. I explained how God instructed Israel about the Passover lamb and showed him on his door what they did. Then God said, "When I see the blood, I will pass over this house so nobody will die." I told him that the Jews celebrate this event to this day by celebrating the Passover feast. Hassan said, "Still today?" I said yes.

I then told him that all the true believers of Israel sacrificed animals all the time. God used the animal sacrifices to teach them that He requires a sacrifice for sins. I quoted, "Without the shedding of blood, there can be no remission of sins." I then explained "remission." I then said that the blood of animals could never actually take away sins. But the prophets foretold of a Messiah who would come from God who would die as a sacrifice for sins and it would satisfy God's demand for justice.

I then explained that when Jesus was introduced by the prophet John, John said, "Look, the Lamb of God who takes away the sin of the world." I explained that this was the reason for Jesus coming here in the first place. He came to die so that we might be saved. And when He did die, God accepted his death as full punishment for our sins. He showed this by raising Jesus from the dead three days later in fulfillment of the prophets' words. Now, anyone who believes in their heart that Jesus died this way for them receives remission of sins and eternal life. I told him that Jesus was always obedient and never sinned and this is what qualified him to die as an acceptable sacrifice that God accepted.

Hassan was understanding the gospel but I needed to draw some implications for him personally. I asked him if he thought this seemed like good news, that God would make a way of salvation like this. He said yes. I then said, "This salvation is only offered to those who truly believe that Jesus died in this way for their sins. So, if you were to ever receive the benefit yourself, you would first have to denounce the Islamic teaching that Jesus did not die." Then Hassan paused and said, "I understand." (I could tell that he understood.)

I then told him that there was another important thing he must understand. Jesus came not just to deliver us from the penalty of sin which is hell. He came also to deliver us from slavery to it. Not only are we brought into a new relationship with God (in which He considers us beloved children with no condemnation whatsoever), but He also gives us life from above.

I asked if ever heard the term "born again" and he said no. I then explained regeneration to him to show that all who are true Christians have been born from above and made alive by God's Spirit. Now, we are new creatures that desire to do the things that please God, not as a means to gain heaven. Rather we want to do the things that please God because it is like food to us. We simply find great pleasure doing the things that please God and we abhor sin and consider it greatly harmful and full of death.

I then told him that according to the Bible all people are born slaves to sin and unable to free himself from its control over their lives. I told him that he is a slave to sin and even if he tried with all his might, he would prove my point. He would fail to live righteously in God's sight. I said that all who have been born again are no longer slaves of sin.

I then asked him if he considered himself a good person and he said yes. I then explained that God considers all people to be evil by nature, not good. I explained that each time Hassan did something that he knew was sin, he actually committed idolatry. He made himself out to be God by acting as if he was the king instead of God. This is vile and we all are guilty.

I paused and said, "Most young Muslim boys I meet your age have their minds on things like their future career, getting married, enjoying life, etc." Hassan said, "I don't look at life this way. I see things as if this is all temporary and things are getting bad." I told him that this was God's mercy at work making him see things that many people do not see.

I then took out a tract and a gospel of John (GOJ) and gave it to him. He asked if the GOJ was from the beginning of the Bible and I pointed to where it is found by using my full Bible. I told him that he could use the tract to remember what we discussed. I also said that I might come back again in 3 weeks or so to see if he read the GOJ. If he says yes, I would them present a full Bible to him and ask him if he would like to have it as a gift. I asked if this would be okay and he said yes.

I then quoted Jesus, "Seek and you shall find." I said that if you are sincerely concerned about these matters, nothing prevents you from asking God to show you what is true and what He wants for you. I also told him that I would be praying.

Note: We went back on three occasions to talk with Hassan. Every time, the person who came to the door told us that Hassan is not home. But they acted as if they were withholding information from us. On the third visit back, his brother came to the door. Again, he seemed very evasive. He said that Hussan no longer lives there. As we talked, Hussan's father came to the door. I told him that I was a Christian who talked with Hussan a few weeks ago. The man looked very distant but his English was just fine. He seemed to be hiding something. He said that Hussan went to Iraq. But then he said he went up north here in Michigan. I don't think we will find out what actually happened. But we have noticed that often, after explaining the gospel to a teenager, something occurs afterwards behind the scene. I know of one case in which one teenage Iraqi was sent back to Iraq after he told his parents that he wanted to be a Christian. May God watch over Hussan and lead him to other Christians wherever he might be currently living.

Godda: Lebanese Muslim woman. We gave an Eng/Arabic N.T. and tracts to Godda to give to her mother. (We met her mother a few weeks earlier.)

Godda told us that various people have been coming to the house lately. We found out that they were most likely JW people.   To differentiate, we told Godda that the main point of our message has to do with God's justice. To illustrate, I said that according to the Bible, if she were to live her entire life without sin except for one little lie and then died with just that one little lie, God would have no choice but to send her to hell forever. She winced and said that they believe God is merciful.

I told her that we also believe that God is merciful but He cannot excuse sin. It must all be punished because He is absolute in his justice/righteousness. She assumed that we were saying something else....that God punishes for a time in hell until each person's sin is punished. But I said, no...hell is forever. In order to extend mercy without compromising his absolute righteousness, God made a way to save sinners through a substitute sacrifice. This is what the entire Bible is all about.

I explained the animal sacrifices to demonstrate that God's demand for sacrifice has always been known. But they were just pictures because the blood of animals can never actually take away sins. So, He came here Himself by miracle as a man in order to die as a substitute sacrifice. When Jesus died, God accepted His death as full payment for sin. Now, anyone who believes that Jesus died for their sins personally in this way receives remission of sins and eternal life. But this does not apply to anyone who insists that Jesus did not die.

Godda said, "We believe that Jesus died." I told her that I had only met a handful of Muslims who believe that Jesus actually died. She said that they believe He did. But then she said that the two religions were very similar. So, I told her that on this point, they are opposite. I said that many of the teachings of Islam are antichrist and insulting to Jesus. For example, if any person thinks that they might be accepted by God on the basis of their own goodness, he makes Jesus' death out to be of no value. After all, if I can make it without Jesus' payment, who needs his death? Godda began to understand intellectually what I meant by Islam being antichrist.

I then told her that there is another teaching that most Muslims do not know. I said, "Jesus came not just to deliver us from the penalty of sin, but also from slavery to it." I then gave her my testimony to explain regeneration and how God makes us into new creatures who obey Him happily because they love him. They don't have to do things in order to obtain God's acceptance. They agree with God that they deserve hell forever. But they believe that Jesus already paid for their sin. Now, they do the things that please God because they enjoy pleasing him. God has put his Spirit inside us and He is the one who deserves all the credit for the good things that we do.

Godda understood the things we told her but unless God causes her to remember them and then also causes the gospel to begin to stir inside her, she will go on living as she has been living and perish. With all the attention being given by false teachers coming to them, I suspect that there is a spiritual battle being waged in heavenly places.

Hassan (Lebanese Muslim man about 30 years old). Muhammad, his father, was also present but he could not speak English. It was absolutely clear to both Linda and me that the Holy Spirit attended this meeting. He gave Hassan the ability to understand quickly and He caused the gospel to be articulated with the greatest clarity. It seemed to me that He was the one speaking. The evidence of this cannot be communicated in this report. You had to be there to experience it for yourself. Though it did not seem taxing at the time, after going door to door I was extremely exhausted.

Hassan and his family just arrived in the U.S. within the past year. He is a pharmacist. After we introduced ourselves, I askde if he had any interest in talking about the way to heaven. He paused and then opened the door so we could come in to sit. We had some small talk in the beginning just to get acquainted. I told him we were evangelical Christians. He did not know that term. I said we were not Catholic. We are Protestant. He understood this term.

I then told Hassan that the things we came to talk about are things that most Christians do not seem to talk about very much so he will probably learn things he never knew before. I said that we want most of all to explain about a certain characteristic of God. I asked if he ever heard the word "righteousness." He asked if there was another word that means about the same thing. I said, "Justice." He understood this word.

I said that God is a judge and He must hold up justice in the most strict way. He cannot let any sin go unpunished. I said, "Pretend that you lived your entire life without sinning except once you made a little lie. Then, you died with just that one little lie and went to the judgment. According to the Bible, God would have to send you to hell forever because He cannot have any sin whatsoever come to him." A little smile came over his face and he said, "So then, everyone is going to hell?" I smiled back and said that I was happy that he understood what I was saying. I said that indeed, everyone is headed for hell but because God is merciful, He made a way of escape. But it is important to understand first that God cannot let a single sin go unpunished because his justice is perfect. He must punish all sin.

But because He is merciful, He made a way for us to be saved. He sent his Son Jesus here to take the punishment as a sacrifice for sins. I then explained the animal sacrifices to show that God has always been communicating that sin must be punished. The man lays his hand on the head of the sheep and then cuts the throat of the sheep. The man's sins figuratively transfer to the sheep. The sheep dies so the man does not have to die. But the blood of animals cannot take away sin. They only picture that God demands a sacrifice for sin. Without the shedding of blood, there can be no forgiveness.

Before He created the world, God planned to send His Son here to die as a sacrifice for sin. This is what the Bible is all about. Because God so loved the world, He sent his only begotten son to die so that all who believe in Him should not perish, but have everlasting life. God takes all their sins and charges them to Jesus. So, our sins were punished on Jesus. And God accepted Jesus' death as full payment for our sins. Now, because the sins were punished, God can forgive the sins of all people who believe that Jesus died in this way to take their punishment. Hassan then put the essential gospel truth about Jesus' substitute death into his own words showing the he understood what we said and that it made sense to him. (The idea of a substitute sacrifice so that God can forgive and without that sacrifice, He cannot forgive.)

I then asked him if he thought that since Jesus paid already, there is no motivation for Christians to live holy lives. Actually, he had not been thinking this way while we were talking but he had heard this concept from other Muslims.

I said that most of the people who call themselves Christian are probably not actually Christian. But all those who are true Christians believe that everyone deserves to go to hell forever because all people are all bad in the sight of God. I spent a few minutes elaborating on this. I said also that when Adam and Eve disobeyed God, sin entered the world and caused all people from that point on to become corrupted. The Bible teaches that we are all born dead to God and slaves to sin. No matter how religious a person might be, he is still a slave to sin. He cannot make himself pure or master over sin.

But Jesus came not just to deliver us from the penalty of sin. He came also to deliver us from the slavery to sin. I then explained regeneration to him to show that nobody really wants God ruling over their lives. We all seek satisfaction and pleasure as we see fit. This is rebellion. But while we were dead, God breathed life into us (the true Christians) and made us spiritually alive to him. He has caused us to be born again. All true Christians have been made alive this way by God's power.

The idea of being able to sin since Jesus already paid for it does not enter into our minds at all. Because God has made us alive to Him, we are changed. We now have an intense hatred for sin and battle against it. Mere religious people cannot have victory over sin because they have only their own power. But because God has made us alive to him, we now truly love him and know him. Our desire is to please him as a son desires to please his father. And our relationship with Him is never in jeopardy because all of our sin has been paid for. God loves us no matter what. But because we truly love him, we are driven out of love to obey him.

I told Hassan that God did not have to do all of this. It is a gift He gave. As a result, we must not take his gift lightly. If we reject his gift, it is a very big insult.

Hassan spoke up and said, "It is very good that you are doing what you are doing. I never heard these things before. I am glad that you came here today to explain all this." We gave him tracts and a GOJ/R and told him about out meetings. He said he would like us to come back and talk more after he reads the gospel. (We did go back but he was busy studying for his certification. We plan to go back again soon.)

Muhammad, Muslim Iraqi in his later 30's. After we introduced ourselves, we asked him if he would be interested to talk with us about the way to heaven. He said, "Let us start talking and if it is something I like, we will continue." I told him that there are many people that might come to his door to talk like this but I planned to tell him some things that he most likely has not heard before. I told him that the talk would be about God's justice.

I said that since Muhammad is a Muslim, he already believes that God is a God of justice and that one day, He will bring judgment to all mankind. He agreed. I then said that the way the Bible talks about God's justice is much different than the way of Islam. At about this point, he said that he wanted us to get a couple of chairs from the back yard and then sit under his big tree for shade.

After sitting comfortably in the shade, Muhammad's two brothers pulled up and were asking for tools. I asked them what they all do for a living and one of them said, "Do you have any ideas?" This began a long discussion, mainly with Muhammad about career choices, etc. I was able to tell him many things that I had learned over the years and he seemed appreciative. I also told him that I can provide names of other Christians that might give him further guidance in the areas of his immediate interest. We talked for at least ½ hour about these things and it seemed that Muhammad recognized that I put off my agenda to provide sincere help concerning the things that are heavy on his heart right now.

After that conversation ran its course, I got back to talking about God's justice. I told him that I would give a scenario to illustrate a very important teaching of the Bible. I said that according to the Bible, if Muhammad lived his entire life perfectly without sin except for one little lie and then died with that one little lie only and went to the judgment, God would have no choice but to send him to hell forever. An expression of unbelief came to his face with a little smile added in.

I then said that as a Muslim, I knew he was thinking that God is merciful and what I had just told him does not fit with his view of God. I said that Christians also believe that God is merciful but what I just told him probably seems to contradict this. I said that the Bible portrays God as someone who is not happy to throw people into hell. But it says that He is a God of absolute righteousness and cannot let a single sin go unpunished. I then gave him the illustration of the human judge who fails to uphold justice by letting a murderer go free simply because that murder felt remorse and was sorry for what he did. I explained that such a human judge failed to do his job. He failed to uphold the law. I said that God is not like that human judge who lets the guilty go unpunished. In order to provide a way that the guilty could be forgiven, He had to make a way of doing so while still punishing the sins.

Then I discussed the animal sacrifices to talk about the concept of substitution in the Bible. I also conveyed the story of the Passover to him to show that God has always been communicating this concept. Then I said that on the night He was betrayed, Jesus was celebrating the Passover feast with His friends. Then He took the bread and broke it and said, "This is my body that is broken for you, from now on, do this in remembrance of me." He said the same thing with the cup relating it to his blood that would soon be shed for them signifying the new covenant that God is making. I said that when the prophet John introduced Jesus, he said, "Look. The Lamb of God who takes away the sin of the world!" I said that long before Jesus was born, the prophets foretold of a Messiah who would come for the express purpose of dying as a substitute lamb so sinners could be reconciled to God.

I told him that God is holy and cannot have any sin whatsoever come to him. The sins had to be punished. An animal sacrifice would not do because the blood of animals can never take away sins. And if I were to die for Muhammad, that would not satisfy God's righteous demands either because I am a sinner just like Muhammad. But Jesus came here, took upon human flesh and lived always in complete obedience to His Father. When He voluntarily gave up his life on the cross, God showed that He accepted this as payment in full by raising Jesus from the dead. Now, the gospel promise is this. If anyone believes that Jesus died in this way bearing his sins, he receives remission of sins and eternal life.

On two or three occasions during our talk, Muhammad tried to explain a concept of Islam that he thought related to the discussion. Each time, after he explained the point, I told him that I was aware of this teaching but I would then get back to the discussion. He was perceiving that I had already heard the teaching and found no merit whatsoever in it. These exchanges were polite. There was no debating. I told him that I was there not to debate but to provide information from the Bible to him. He recognized that there was no reason to try debating with us because our minds were obviously settled.

The last subject I covered had to do with regeneration. I told him that all people are born slaves to sin and do not have the power to break that bondage. So, because we believe the Bible, we fully believe that Muhammad is a slave to sin and unable to free himself from its grip. I told him that there are only two types of people. Those who believe God and those who don't. A man can be very religious but not believe God. Someone who believes God believes what God has said about Himself and about what God has declared about all mankind...that we deserve to go to hell forever. Down through time, there have been only a few by comparison who believe God. For example, Abraham believed God and God declared him righteous. But the Bible teaches that God could not declare Abraham righteous just because he believed God. The death of Jesus 2000 years later made it possible for God to declare Abraham righteous. Abraham's sins were punished on Jesus.

Why did Abraham believe God and so many others not believe Him? It is because God made Abraham spiritually alive. Jesus said, "Unless a man is born again, he will not see the Kingdom of heaven." People like Abraham, David, Moses, Linda and me....we have been made alive by God. We have been born again." I told him that Muhammad is a slave to sin just like we used to be slaves to sin. But now, the Bible says that we are no longer slaves to sin.

I then told him my testimony with Linda there to verify it. She also said things that illustrated that once, we were spiritually dead and wanted nothing to do with God's rule over our lives. But God made us alive and has been changing us more and more over time. Now, we desire to do the things that please God. We do them not to gain entrance to heaven. Jesus already paid for that. We do it because we enjoy doing the things that please God. He made us into new people.

I asked Muhammad, "Does all of this sound like good news to you?" Linda noticed a change in his expression. Then he said yes. He then asked, "What should I do next?"

Now some of you might object to how I handed his question because I did not tell him to repeat a prayer. After all, it was as if he was saying, "What must I do to be saved?"

I took out my tract and a gospel and handed it to him. I then told him that the Bible teaches God can make people come to new life in Christ as they learn and meditate on this gospel message. If he is really interested, he owes it to himself to learn it well and meditate upon it. He agreed to read it and asked me if he could call me and what time is best. We exchange telephone numbers. He then asked, can you come back again to talk more and I assured him that I already planned to do that. I told him that I am available as much as he wants me to be available.

He asked if there was anything else he should do. I told him that if he is sincere about this, he should begin asking God to open up his eyes so he can see his sin the way God sees it. I told him that whenever God does this for someone, that person always begins to value more and more what Jesus did by dying for his sins.

Just to make sure he understood, I told him that the salvation Jesus came to bring requires that you believe that Jesus did actually die. If you reject this, you cannot be saved.

I do plan to tell Muhammad over and over that he must repent of his way of living and follow Jesus. I did tell him that when he does this, people will hate him. Jesus said, "If they hated me, they will hate you."

I said about as much as I thought I was supposed to say to Muhammad on that first visit. I do not have to worry or wonder whether I was supposed to tell Muhammad to do this or that. I also do not have to worry if I failed and put Muhammad's soul in danger by not doing so. Here is what I know. If God is at work to save Muhammad, God will indeed cause Muhammad to begin trembling about his soul. As he reads the gospel, his fear and desire for the living waters will increase and there will be no stopping Muhammad in his pursuit of salvation.

Though I am fully confident that nothing can stop God from bringing the gospel to new life in Muhammad, I do not let this knowledge deter me from fervent prayer for him. If we don't pray, we should not expect God to save Muhammad...period.

Muhammad update:

After our initial conversation with Muhammad (above), I began meeting with him weekly. I have spent many hours with him studying the Bible and teaching him the gospel. I learned that other Christians have also been talking with him for years about the gospel. He seemed all eager to learn and persistently asked to meet. He came to a few of our meetings. But it seems as if his interest is all talk. I have begun to seriously wonder about his motives for meeting in the first place. After six months of meeting with Muhammad, it was clear that Muhammad was not inclined to be serious about following Jesus.

Then, at Muhammad's request, I met again with him and the results of that meeting are provided below. I want you to know ahead of time that I normally do not say things this harsh. Certainly, I do not normally talk about Islam. I prefer to stick to the gospel of Jesus. But I wanted to include this conversation to demonstrate that we must not shy away from proclaiming the truth. And in some situations, it may be time to offer stern rebuke.

Muhammad   This is the Iraqi Muslim (about 40 years old).

Yesterday morning, before going out, I received a call from a good brother who called to remind me that when we go out, we go out with the authority of Jesus who told us to go. It was not long after that call that Muhammad called me and asked if I would come over to his house. I told him that I would call him back about it. (I did not know yet if I was going door to door or just doing follow up visits.) At about noon, I found out that nobody would be going, including my wife because of a health situation. Then she asked what I planned to do. I told her that I would probably do follow up visits. Then she said, "Maybe you should go see Muhammad." She said that God had put it in her heart to pray for him a few hours earlier. So, I called him and set up the visit.

When I arrived, Muhammad was not home because he had been called to go help someone. So, I proceeded to do other follow up visits. After doing them, Muhammad called me and told me he was back home so I went to his house.

When I first arrived, he had several questions about running a new electrical circuit in his living room. I wondered if this was all he wanted from me. But after 30 minutes of explanation, we went to the basement and talked.

He said, "You have told me that if I was to become a follower of Jesus, I must be willing to lose everything, right?" (When he said this, I wondered if perhaps he was seriously contemplating the idea of following Jesus.) I told him that Jesus did say, "Unless a man is willing to die for me, he cannot be my disciple." So, yes, you must be willing to lose everything if need be for Jesus' sake.

Muhammad then said, "Put yourself in my place. What if God were to suddenly tell you that the things you have been believing were all incorrect and then He asked you to change what you thought and go another way and that when you do, you could lose everything dear to you. Would you change?" I told him that I would do anything that God wants me to do and if He were ever to show me error, I would change my thinking.

Muhammad breathed deeply as if relieved. Then he asked me if I have ever considered the message of the Karan. This came as a surprise since we have already discussed this completely. But since he asked me to come over and he was the one to ask, I answered him and in hindsight, I believe that God answered him with words of serious rebuke.

It was if God took over the control of my mouth and the words poured out. I told him that the Karan is antichrist and it is an evil book that is sending millions of people to hell with a message to purposely deceive and blind people from the gospel. Actually, this is merely a summary of this portion of the discussion because the actual time spent ripping Islam was about 10 minutes. Muhammad just sat there with his mouth open. I imagine he considered everything I said to be highly insulting.

I then told him that he is headed to hell. God has mercifully brought him His message of peace bought by the death of His only Son. Muhammad attempted to make an earthly illustration that depicted Jesus merely as a prophet who did many wonderful things before the evil leaders put a stop to it. In his description of Jesus, Muhammad kept avoiding the death of Jesus and harped on all the other things Jesus did. But with each thing Muhammad said, I kept saying, "And HE DIED." Then Muhammad told me that he loves Jesus.

I then told Muhammad that he loves a false idea of Jesus, not the real Jesus. He hates the real Jesus and is spitting in Jesus' face by rejecting the gift of eternal life He died to bring. I told him that Jesus considers him an enemy.

I then told him that he insults God to even think for one second that he is good enough to stand in God's presence. I told him he is not good but evil through and through. He is unclean in the sight of God and headed directly to hell.

After several minutes of this talk, I stood up and told Muhammad that it is best now to conclude our meeting. I told him that I would understand if Muhammad considers the things I said insulting but I must tell the truth rather than shy away from it. Muhammad told me that he knows that I have always been telling him these things.

At the door, just before leaving, I stopped and told Muhammad that he should try to think of me as a prophet, not as one of the prophets like Abraham. But then again, very much like that. Like a prophet, God sent me to you to speak His message to you. And you have not been listening. Then I left. (We are still friends I think.)

End of sample gospel conversations.

Appendix H: It is Better to Say "Remission" (of Sins) Than "Forgiveness" (of Sins)

"To Him all the prophets witness that, through His name, whoever believes in Him will receive __remission__ of sins" (Acts 10:43).

Most modern versions use the word **forgiveness** in this verse rather than the word **remission**. I believe the word forgiveness in its base meaning is a suitable choice of words. In spite of this, I recommend that we use the less common word remission (of sins) whenever we are explaining the gospel. Normally, I like to use words that are more commonly understood than words that people are less likely to understand. But this is an exception.

I admit that if you use the phrase "remission of sins" instead of "forgiveness of sins," most people will not understand what you are saying. If you use the word remission, you will have to pause for a moment and define the word for the hearer. At this point, you might be thinking to yourself, "Why use a word that I must then define?....Why not just use the word "forgiveness" since most people understand the basic concept of forgiveness?"

I hope to show here that when you use the word "forgiveness," you will most likely fail to properly communicate the concept of what God wants communicated. The problem is not the word itself (forgiveness). It is the unbeliever's false comprehension of the word forgiveness that introduces the error in the minds of those who hear it. Some people have a more distorted understanding of the concept of forgiveness than others. But I maintain that almost everyone has a distorted understanding of it.

To illustrate the basic problem, let me explain what seems to be the mindset of most Muslims concerning the concept of forgiveness. Muslims call their sins "mistakes." Obviously, this thinking grossly diminishes the ugliness of their sin and reduces their likelihood of recognizing their need of salvation. But in addition to this distortion about their sin, they also have a diminished view of God's absolute righteousness which cannot tolerate any sin whatsoever. With such crippled understanding of these important matters, they are hindered from understanding the gospel, including the concept of forgiveness.

These corrupt views, together with their own experience of forgiving others (such as their children for example), are mingled together in their minds to form a corrupt understanding of the concept of forgiveness. Because of these things, to the Muslim, if God forgives, He is simply overlooking the "mistakes." So, if we use the phrase forgiveness of sins when talking with a Muslim, he thinks you mean that God will "overlook" mistakes. Hopefully you recognize that this is a gross distortion of the gospel.

Because we want to communicate the gospel as clearly as we can, I suggest it is best to avoid using the phrase "forgiveness of sins" when explaining the gospel to Muslims. But I would go further and suggest that it would be better to avoid using this phrase when talking with any unbeliever. Most likely, every unbeliever you encounter has a distorted understanding of the concept of forgiveness. To some degree, most unbelievers understand it to be God overlooking our faults. This is not how this concept is defined by the New Testament.

Remission actually conveys the biblical view of what happens when a person repents and believes the gospel. It conveys the idea of the sins being sent away or removed, not merely overlooked. When this occurs, a person is "reconciled" to God. The reconciliation is made possible by the legal removal of sins.

When this occurs, God's disposition towards us is forever changed. The Holy God can now bring us near Himself because our sins have been utterly removed. The finished work of Jesus on the cross made this possible. The sins were completely punished. There is no overlooking them! Overlooking them would not be righteous. They had to be fully punished and that is what happened while Jesus hung on the cross. It is completely righteous (just) for God to send our sins away from us. It is not a mere pardon! It is completely righteous for God to declare us righteous (justified).

If we persist in using the word forgiveness, these truths will be obscured because of the person's distorted understanding of forgiveness. So, even though the average person does not understand what the word remission means, it is probably the better term to use when you are trying to help them understand the gospel properly. Yes, you will have to stop to define the word remission, but that process will actually call attention to the rich truth of what occurred when Jesus hung on the cross.

Other Books Written by Tom Bear

To obtain these books, go to Thomas Bear's author page on Amazon.

Overcoming the Powers of Darkness -Using God's Spiritual Armor. It is the goal of our enemy to lull us into an apathetic, lukewarm spiritual existence. To obtain the abundant life, we cannot sit back passively and wait for God to spiritually zap us. We must engage in spiritual battle. In his epistle to the Ephesians, the Apostle Paul used imagery of a soldier's armor. Some have suggested that we engage in spiritual battle by mentioning the various pieces of this armor in a daily prayer. This is not true. Paul was teaching about spiritual principles that we must employ as a way of life. This book examines these spiritual principles and provides strong exhortation to increase our desire to live the abundant life that Jesus offers to us. (133 pages in paperback edition.)

The Gospel Guide to Safe Harbor for Your Soul- How to Become a Disciple of Jesus Christ: This book is written to help those who are concerned about what will happen to them after they die. Ideally, a Christian friend will use to this book to help those who want to learn to follow Jesus Christ. But even without such a friend, this book can still guide people through this process. This book unashamedly teaches that the gospel of Jesus Christ is THE WAY and the only way of salvation that God has provided. It does not attempt to argue, debate or prove it. It merely proclaims it as true and presents it as the remedy all people need. There are three standalone parts: Part One: Learn the gospel and come to agreement with it. -Part Two: The appropriate response to the gospel. -Part Three: Your ongoing response to the gospel. Readers should progress through this book one part at a time and at their own pace. At the end of each part, there are a few questions that can be answered from the material covered in that part. Answers to these questions are available in the back of the book. By God's grace, readers will learn the gospel of Jesus Christ and then become disciples of Jesus Christ and eventually spend eternity with Him. This book can help parents guide their children to the way of salvation. Also, Christians can help their unbelieving friends learn how to become a disciple of Jesus by giving them a copy of this book.

Evangelism Fuel- Motivation to Evangelize: Does it seem like your evangelism light has diminished? The wonder and beauty of Jesus forms the basis of a bright witness of Jesus Christ in this world. This type of witness requires the supernatural power of the Holy Spirit to be unleashed in us. It is not something that we can produce in our own strength. The Holy Spirit must be freely moving in us to produce a life that experiences the power and person of Jesus Christ. As we come in contact with His glory in this way, we will have much reason and motivation to testify to the wonder of Jesus. This book is written in a devotional style with short, heart-felt meditations that can be read in just a few minutes each day. These meditations are intended to help believers understand the supernatural work God calls them to do and motivate them to seek and experience God's glory in it. (110 pages in paperback format.)

The Way to Heaven- The Difference Between Islam and Christianity: Tom Bear has been an evangelical Christian since 1975. During the past several years, he has spoken with thousands of Muslims face to face, one on one, at great length about their understanding of God and the gospel of Jesus Christ. This book is based upon this experience and his understanding of the gospel of Jesus Christ. Like many people, you may be under the impression that the Bible and the Koran generally teach that to get to heaven, a person must achieve a certain level of "goodness" by doing more good things than bad things. In reality, each teach an opposing view about the way to heaven. This book is written to explain the difference between these two messages while attempting to explain how most Muslims I meet think about this matter. This book is an excellent gift for any Muslim who sincerely wants to learn the gospel of Jesus. (100 Pages in paperback edition)

The Local Church: Most pastors wish that the members of their churches would grow and flourish more. The church members often sense that God has purposes for them but they don't know what He wants them to do. They often end up playing the role of an unfulfilled spectator. *The Local Church* examines the early New Testament Church and its teachings for answers to this universal problem. It demonstrates how certain unbiblical attitudes and traditions exist which cultivate this unhealthy spectator mindset. *The Local Church* challenges leaders and "laypeople" to identify and discard these unbiblical attitudes and practices that stifle spiritual health. This book asserts that if the pattern of the early New Testament Church is followed today, Christians will mature at a greater pace and experience fulfillment as active participants in the advancement of Christ's Kingdom. (160 pages in paperback edition)

The Christian and Habitual Sin: Jesus said that He came to give abundant life. Does this characterize your life? Or does it seem like you are in bondage to sinful attitudes or behaviors? The Apostle Paul warned that people whose lifestyles are controlled by sexual addiction, substance addiction, habitual overeating, jealousy, hostility or anger will not inherit the Kingdom of Heaven. (See Galatians 5:19-21.) These behaviors and attitudes directly contradict the life Jesus came to give. Anyone whose life is dominated by them cannot have peace if he is a Christian. The author was at one time addicted to very powerful drugs and sexual sins but has found deliverance through Jesus Christ. He wrote this book to help other Christians gain sustained deliverance through the application of biblical instruction, not based upon theory, but proven through his own experience. It is intentionally brief so it can be read in less than one hour. *This book is a helpful counseling tool for pastors and good to give to any Christian struggling with habitual sin.* (60 pages in paperback edition)

Bring My Sheep Back! (Church Discipline, the Loving Way) presents a candid framework for the process of restoring Christians that stray. Most of the books that deal with this subject approach it from the standpoint of solving conflicts between Christians. *Bring My Sheep Back* is founded on Jesus' teaching to put the interests of the straying Christian ahead of our own desire for immediate relief of pain caused by the one caught in sin. Personal observations along with much attention to biblical instruction produce a very useful and thorough resource for church leaders and lay people who desire to restore Christians trapped by sin. This book warns against dependence on man-made approaches to solving relational problems. Whether it involves private sin or public scandal, or even cases that involve the governing authorities, biblical principles are taught as foundational to the process of restoration. (130 pages in paperback edition)

Birth Control: A Spiritual Shackle- Did you know that before the twentieth century, the Protestant Church boldly spoke out against the practice of birth control? They were opposed to any act of man that interfered with the natural order of procreation. Men such as John Calvin, Martin Luther, John Wesley, Arthur Pink and Augustine were vehemently opposed to birth control. Today, Birth control is not just tolerated, it is embraced by the Protestant Church. Why has the Protestant Church changed its position? Is it possible that Christians living before the twentieth century were all mistaken? Why did they take a stand against birth control? Is it possible that the church of the nineteenth century was better equipped to discern right from wrong? Using six biblical arguments, this book demonstrates that birth control is a worldly practice that opposes God's will for His people, violates the marriage covenant and is an attack on the very character of God. (70 pages in paperback edition)

Christian Marriage: This book explains biblical principles that if applied, will result in marital harmony and glory to God. The premise of this book is that all problems in Christian marriages are the result of a failure to live as the Bible teaches us to live. This book examines the biblical role of the husband and the wife and instruction about resolving marital conflict God's way. *Christian Marriage* is an excellent **marital counseling resource** for couples planning to marry and also for those who seek restoration of their marriage. It has served some couples for years as a valued reference book.

Toward the Celestial City- The Lives of Tom and Linda Bear: We look like ordinary people who live in an ordinary home in an ordinary neighborhood. If you read this book, you will conclude that our lives have NOT been ordinary. On the one hand, you will read how two people made such an extraordinary mess of their lives resulting in hopeless drug addiction and an utterly ruined marriage. On the other hand, you will see how God transformed all of the garbage that we created into a glorious display of His love and power. *"Behold, I make all things new."* As you read our story, you will find some things astounding, some miraculous, some hilarious, some things uplifting and some things sad. This book bears witness to the fact that God continually makes Himself known to His children though the things He does and the way He does them. *"The works of the LORD are great, studied by all who have pleasure in them" (Psalm 111:2).* If it were not for His loving, providential involvement in every aspect of our lives, we would **only know about Him** and we would not actually **know Him personally**. It is our hope that this book will allow the reader to see how God has made Himself known to us personally through the events and circumstances of our lives. We believe you will be encouraged as you read about the many awesome answers to prayer which clearly demonstrate that God is powerful and actively working in the lives of His children.

10400662R00099

Made in the USA
Lexington, KY
21 September 2018